AMERICA
IN RUINS

"[*America in Ruins*] reflects growing concern among a wide range of officials about what they call the nation's infrastructure. . . . Half to two-thirds of the nation's cities and other communities would be unable to support modernized development without large investments in streets, roads, bridges, water and sewer systems, waste disposal sites, treatment plants, and other facilities."

The New York Times

"The most thoughtful and trenchant document in existence on the role of public works in a vital society. . . . With an economy of words and the use of supporting but nonobfuscating statistical evidence, Choate and Walter have conceived the blueprint for economic and social revitalization. . . . Every board member and senior officer of a private sector organization should be given a copy of this book, and, if possible, asked to take an examination on its conclusions. For public policy officers not to study it is highest folly."

Corporate Public Issues

"An eloquent warning against the rise of 'the throwaway society' that would allow the slow ruin of its cities. . . . *America in Ruins* is a truly comprehensive review of the state of the nation's cities today. With the potential to create the public awareness that can stimulate the rebuilding of the nation's urban infrastructure, it may become one of the most important books of the decade."

Congressman James Oberstar (D-Minn.)

Other books to be published in cooperation with The Council of State Planning Agencies, edited and with a new introduction by Michael Barker, with a foreword by Robert N. Wise:

> *State Employment Policy in Hard Times*
> *Financing State Economic Development*
> *State Taxation Policy and Economic Growth*
> *Rebuilding the American Infrastructure*
>   (including *America in Ruins* and two new essays)

The Council of State Planning Agencies is a membership organization comprised of the planning and policy staff of the nation's governors. Through its Washington office, the Council provides assistance to individual states on a wide spectrum of policy matters. The Council also performs policy and technical research on both state and national issues. The Council was formed in 1966; it became affiliated with The National Governors' Association in 1975.

Published in cooperation with
The Council of State Planning Agencies

AMERICA IN RUINS

The Decaying Infrastructure

Pat Choate and Susan Walter

Duke Press Paperbacks   Durham, N.C. 1983

Reprinted with permission by Duke University Press as a facsimile of the original edition. The views and findings contained in this volume are those of the authors, and do not necessarily represent those of the members or staff of The Council of State Planning Agencies or any of its affiliated organizations.

Library of Congress Cataloging in Publication Data

Choate, Pat.
  America in ruins.

  (Duke Press paperbacks)
  Reprint. Originally published: Washington, D.C.:
Council of State Planning Agencies, 1981.
  Bibliography: p.
  1. United States—Public works. I. Walter, Susan.
II. Title. III. Series.
HD3887.C47 1983   363'.0973   82–20963
ISBN 0–8223–0554–2 (pbk.)

PUBLISHER'S FOREWORD

"America's public facilities are wearing out faster than they are being replaced." That is the essential message of this remarkable book which strikes at the heart of a national problem long ignored, the decaying of America's infrastructure.

"We are undermining efforts to revitalize the economy and threatening, in hundreds of communities, the continuation of such basic services as fire protection, public transportation, and water supplies," say the authors.

At first, it appeared theirs was a voice in the wilderness. But today, after *America in Ruins* has received front page coverage on several occasions in the *New York Times*, has been a cover story in *Time* and *Newsweek*, and has been the subject of major legislative debate in the U.S. Congress, we believe it is time for all Americans to take a close look at this book's startling conclusions.

The authors assert that "the United States is seriously underinvesting in public infrastructure. . . . for at least two decades, in both the public and private sectors, we have favored consumption over investment." Apparently we have a genuine crisis on our hands. But what do we intend to do about it?

"It would be all too tempting to . . . assume that public works expenditures must be drastically curtailed in the face of current economic conditions," the authors contend. They go on to say, "Such a course would contravene the very purposes of the economic renewal programs now being formulated."

Duke University Press, with its deep concern for public policy issues, is indebted to The Council of State Planning Agencies, which made possible this publication, and to the expertise of the authors, Pat Choate and Susan Walter. We offer it exactly as it has been circulated to a select group of federal, state, and local officials and planners, and in the same hard-hitting report form.

ACKNOWLEDGEMENTS

The various drafts of this book have been reviewed by many individuals. Since many of these people are in government positions, to list them would take advantage of their frankness and contributions. However, their thoughtful and often provocative suggestions are appreciated.

Several individuals within our respective organizations were most helpful, including Robert Wise and Patrick Henry. We are particularly appreciative of the time, attention, ideas and suggestions of Ralph Widner, Michael Barker and Ken Rainey.

More than is usually the case, the reviewers of these drafts should be absolved of any responsibilities for the recommendations made at several points in this work since they often disagreed. Although several sections were revised in response to their comments, they may feel these modifications were insufficient.

The initial drafts of this work were carefully edited by Lois Malone. Her ability to bring clarity and simplicity from our initial drafts is both appreciated and admired. The work of Carol Simon in preparing this piece for final publication was most helpful. Her attention to detail continues to impress us.

Norma de Freitas, Cathy Lefevre and Pam Norris made contributions far beyond the typing of the many drafts of this work. Their promptness and good spirit made a significant contribution to the timely publication of this book.

We most appreciate the support given to us by Diane C. Choate and J. Jackson Walter, our spouses. We are sure they wished this work was finished long before it was. Their good humor and encouragement helped us very much.

As always the authors assume sole responsibility for any errors of fact or interpretation contained in this book.

CONTENTS

TABLES

CHARTS

SUMMARY AND INTRODUCTION

America's public facilities are wearing out faster than they are being replaced. Under the exigencies of tight budgets and inflation, the maintenance of public facilities essential to national economic renewal has been deferred. Replacement of obsolescent public works has been postponed. New construction has been cancelled.

The deteriorated condition of basic facilities that underpin the economy will prove a critical bottleneck to national economic renewal during this decade unless we can find ways to finance public works.

It is possible so long as we are not tempted to fall back upon ineffective tinkering. Wholesale revolution is not necessary either. But it does mean that the Executive Branch must share responsibility for creating and managing public works policy more coherently than in the past.

Congress should require the preparation of a *Special Analysis* to accompany each annual budget outlining the nation's public works needs as they affect national economic performance.

Congress should direct the Executive Branch to undertake an inventory of national public works needs as they affect the economy.

With the inventory as a starting point, Congress should then require preparation of a Capital Budget that proposes phased capital investments matched to both short-term cyclical and long-term national economic needs. The budget would display preconstruction, construction, maintenance, and operating costs.

Congress should direct the Executive Branch to report by an appropriate date steps by means of which delays in public facilities construction can be reduced through reforms in federal, state, and local administrative procedures. Similar efforts in reducing other regulatory delays are already underway at the direction of the President.

Congress and the Executive Branch should consider undertaking a series of reforms designed to minimize corruption and waste connected with public works expenditures.

The Executive Branch should undertake an administrative evaluation of the scattered public works activities of the federal government and be prepared to consumate consolidated reforms simultaneously with the proposed Public Works Report to Congress.

Congress or the Executive Branch should direct the Advisory Commission on Intergovernmental Relations or a new body constituted for the purpose to review the public works responsibilities of each level of government and propose appropriate guidelines for allocating functions and responsibilities.

It would be all too tempting to avoid the difficulties of disentangling the knotted threads of intergovernmental complexity and to assume that federal public works expenditures must be drastically curtailed in the face of current economic conditions. But such a course would contravene the very purposes of economic policy now being formulated.

Economic renewal must be the premier focus of domestic policy in this decade. Our public infrastructure is strategically bound-up in that renewal. Without attention to deterioration of that infrastructure, economic renewal will be thwarted if not impossible.

We have no recourse but to face the complex task at hand of rebuilding our public facilities as an essential prerequisite to economic renewal.

1

DETERIORATING FACILITIES/ DECLINING INVESTMENTS

America's public facilities are wearing out faster than they are being replaced. The deteriorated condition of the basic public facilities that underpin the economy presents a major structural barrier to the renewal of our national economy. In hundreds of communities, deteriorated public facilities threaten the continuation of basic community services such as fire protection, public transportation, water supplies, secure prisons and flood protection.

The United States is seriously underinvesting in public infrastructure. Because of tight budgets and inflation, the maintenance of a growing number of national and local public facilities has been deferred. Replacement and rehabilitation of obsolescent public works have been postponed. New construction has been cancelled, delayed or "stretched out."

Because the Congress has tended to dominate national public works policy, the Executive Branch of the federal government has failed to produce a capital budget to guide federal public works expenditures. The attention of Congress to public works is fragmented among numerous committees. In turn, the disorder in federal policies and administrative procedures creates major obstacles to effective state and local public works policy-making and management.

Despite a number of recent analyses, the precise condition of the nation's public works inventory—and the future investments we face—remains unknown. While comprehensive and reliable information is still lacking, the partial information that is available paints a disturbing picture:

■ The nation's 42,500-mile Interstate Highway System, only now approaching completion, is deteriorating at a rate requiring reconstruction of 2,000 miles of road per year. Because adequate funding for rehabilitation and reconstruction was not forthcoming in the late 1970s, over 8,000 miles of this system and 13 percent of its bridges are now beyond their designed service life and must be rebuilt.[1] Although the system constitutes less than one percent of the nation's highways, it handles over 20 percent of all highway traffic. Its further decline will adversely affect the national economy and the well-being of thousands of communities and individual firms.

■ The costs of rehabilitation and new construction necessary to maintain existing levels of service on non-urban highways will exceed $700 billion during the 1980s.[2] Even excluding the estimated $75

1

billion required to complete the unconstructed final 1,500 miles of the Interstate System, the balance required for rehabilitation and reconstruction is still greater than *all* the public works investments made by *all* units of government in the 1970s. Since inflation in highway construction has averaged 12.5 percent since 1973 (doubling costs each six years), continuation of present investment levels will permit less than one-third of needs to be met in this decade.[3]

■ One of every five bridges in the United States requires either major rehabilitation or reconstruction. The Department of Transportation has estimated the costs of this task to be as high as $33 billion. Yet in Fiscal Year 1981 Federal Highway Authorizations, only $1.3 billion was allocated to repair bridge deficiencies.[4]

■ Estimates of the amounts required to rebuild the deteriorating road beds and rolling stock of the railroads of the Northeast and Midwest are not available. While economic necessity may compel reductions in CONRAIL trackage by as much as half, or total reorganization of the system itself, this will not obviate the need for rail modernization. Railroads will play a critical role in national efforts to reduce transportation energy consumption and ship more coal to power plants to replace imported oil. This is a national issue of major importance. A viable eastern rail system is essential to the economic health of the western and southern systems since these regional rail systems can thrive only as part of a national network linking all markets and centers of production.

■ No reliable estimates exist of the investments required to modernize our ports, but numerous instances exist of harbor facilities unable to service efficiently world shipping coming to American docks. Vessels in some ports must wait for as long as a month to pick up their cargo.

■ The nation's municipal water supply needs will make heavy demands upon capital markets in the 1980s. The 756 urban areas with populations of over 50,000 will require between $75 billion and $110 billion to maintain their urban water systems over the next 20 years. Approximately one-fifth of these communities will face investment shortfalls, even if present water rates are doubled to produce capital for new investment. At least an additional $10-$13 billion beyond that generated by existing user charges will be required.[5]

■ Over $25 billion in government funds will be required during the next five years to meet existing water pollution control standards.[6]

■ Over $40 billion must be invested in New York City alone over the next nine years to repair, service, and rebuild basic public works facilities that include: 1,000 bridges, two aquaducts, one large water tunnel, several reservoirs, 6,200 miles of paved streets, 6,000 miles of sewers, 6,000 miles of water lines, 6,700 subway cars, 4,500 buses, 25,000 acres of parks, 17 hospitals, 19 city university campuses, 950 schools, 200 libraries, and hundreds of fire houses and police stations.

Because of its fiscal condition, New York City will be able to invest only $1.4 billion per year to repair, service, and rebuild these facilities.[7]

■ At least $1 billion will be required to rebuild Cleveland's basic public works—$250 to $500 million is needed to replace and renovate the publicly-owned water system; over $150 million is required for major repairs of city bridges; and over $340 million must be spent for flood control facilities. In addition to these expenditures, Cleveland must find additional funds to rebuild or resurface 30 percent of its streets, now in a state of advanced deterioration, and to reconstruct the city's sewer collection system, which frequently floods commercial and residential buildings.[8]

■ Even fiscally healthy cities face large public works investment requirements. For example, Dallas must raise almost $700 million for investment in water and sewerage treatment systems in the next nine years. More than $109 million must be generated to repair deteriorating city streets.[9]

■ Over one-half of the nation's 3,500 jails are over 30 years old. At least 1,300 and perhaps as many as 3,000 of these facilities must be either totally rebuilt or substantially rehabilitated in the 1980s.[10] This construction, in most cases, is court ordered. Thus, it often takes legal precedence over most, if not all, other public capital expenditures.

■ Rural facility needs, as yet unknown, are the subject of a major survey by the U.S. Department of Agriculture currently underway.

■ Water resource development will require major investments in *all* regions of the nation in the 1980s. The agricultural base in the old "Dustbowl" will be in jeopardy toward the end of the decade unless new water sources can be developed. After the Second World War, vast underground water resources close to the surface were tapped for irrigation. Today, this area in the Texas and Oklahoma panhandles and surrounding states has over 10 million acres under irrigation (23 percent of the nation's total irrigated farmland). This irrigated production produces over 40 percent of the nation's processed beef and major portions of wheat, sorghums, and other crops that supply much of America's agricultural exports. The region's water source is being depleted. At present rates it will be gone by the year 2000. The reversion of the region's agricultural production back to low-yield dryland farming would have a devastating effect on the economics of six states. It would seriously harm the nation's balance of payments and ultimately reduce the value of the dollar in international markets.[11] If this production is to be retained, major public works to bring surplus water from adjacent regions are required.

Even such water "surplus" areas as New England, Pennsylvania, New Jersey, and New York are in water crises, in part, because of the inadequacies of their water supply, storage, treatment, and distribution systems that become apparent in times in drought.

3

■ A large number of the nation's 43,500 dams require investment to reduce hazardous deficiencies. The Corps of Engineers has already inspected 9,000 of these facilities and found many of them in need of safety improvements. The funds to inspect even the balance of these dams have not been available. A majority of the dams that are potentially hazardous are privately owned and the dam owners lack the financial resources, willingness, or understanding to take remedial measures. Nor do the states have the legislative authority, funds, or trained personnel to conduct their own inspection and remedial efforts.[12]

These are not isolated or extreme examples. They represent broad trends of decline in both the quantity and quality of virtually every type of public works facility in the nation. Unless these trends are reversed—and soon—the number of public facilities in usable condition will fall to even more dangerous levels.

DECLINING INVESTMENT IN PUBLIC WORKS

Since the 1960s, the value of the nation's stock of public works has not been growing. The net value (investment minus straight-line depreciation) of federal public works investments actually declined during eight of the nine years between 1969 and 1977. While the value of state and local investments in public facilities increased during the same period, it was at a declining rate (Table 1).

Traditional investment depreciation techniques are not always an accurate means of accounting for the value of public works. For example, some facilities (such as cast iron water mains) can satisfactorily perform their functions for 100 years or more—and are doing so in many cities. Even when these investments are devalued to zero, they still present a valuable national and community asset.

A more satisfactory means for assessing the condition of our public works is to evaluate the actual quality of services provided by such facilities and their actual condition. Such assessments during the past several years strongly suggest that many public facilities are deteriorating or are inadequate to meet the needs of the coming decade. For example, George Peterson, of the Urban Institute, has assessed the condition of selected public works in nine cities (Baltimore, Dallas, Des Moines, Hartford, New Orleans, Pittsburgh, St. Louis, Seattle, and Newark). Using a 12-level rating system for evaluating the condition of water systems, sewer systems, streets, bridges and mass transit in these cities, (Table 2), this study found some facilities in good condition in each of the cities, but widespread deterioration in most facilities. For example:

1. The mass transit system in each city, with the exception of St. Louis, was found in poor condition.

4

Table 1
Total (residential and non-residential) PWI, Gross and Net, and Depreciation
(millions of constant 1972 dollars)

Year	Federal				State and Local				Total Government			
	Gross Investment[1]	Depreciation	Depreciation As Percent of Gross Investment	Net Investment	Gross Investment[1]	Depreciation	Depreciation As Percent of Gross Investment	Net Investment	Gross Investment[1]	Depreciation	Depreciation As Percent of Gross Investment	Net Investment
1957	3,571	5,395	151.1	-1,824	20,374	8,325	40.86	12,049	23,945	13,720	57.30	10,225
1958	4,364	5,039	115.5	-675	21,663	8,752	40.40	12,911	26,027	13,791	52.99	12,236
1959	3,783	4,679	123.7	-896	22,081	9,128	41.34	12,953	25,864	13,807	53.38	12,057
1960	3,787	4,335	114.5	-548	22,300	9,523	42.70	12,777	26,087	13,858	53.12	12,229
1961	4,424	4,058	91.7	366	23,988	9,929	41.39	14,059	28,412	13,987	49.23	14,425
1962	4,981	3,865	77.6	1,116	24,660	10,342	41.94	14,318	29,641	14,207	47.93	15,434
1963	5,784	3,963	68.5	1,821	26,799	10,780	40.23	16,019	32,583	14,743	45.25	17,840
1964	6,602	3,756	56.9	2,846	28,652	11,259	39.30	17,393	35,254	15,015	42.59	20,239
1965	6,872	3,829	55.7	3,043	30,281	11,775	38.89	18,506	37,153	15,604	42.00	21,549
1966	7,040	3,949	56.1	3,091	32,422	12,327	38.02	20,095	39,462	16,276	41.24	23,186
1967	5,911	4,056	68.6	1,855	35,041	12,933	36.91	22,108	40,952	16,989	41.49	23,963
1968	4,401	4,132	93.9	269	36,944	13,608	36.83	23,336	41,345	17,740	42.91	23,605
1969	3,684	4,170	113.2	-486	34,749	14,277	41.09	20,472	38,433	18,447	48.00	19,986
1970	3,716	4,189	112.7	-473	32,741	14,902	45.51	17,839	36,457	19,091	52.37	17,376
1971	3,931	4,185	106.5	-254	31,882	15,510	48.65	16,372	35,813	19,695	54.99	15,538
1972	4,010	4,164	103.8	-154	31,125	16,111	51.76	15,014	35,135	20,275	57.71	14,860
1973	4,128	4,138	100.2	-10	31,135	16,712	53.68	14,423	35,263	20,850	59.13	14,413
1974	3,845	4,094	106.5	-249	32,147	17,335	53.92	14,812	35,992	21,429	59.54	14,563
1975	3,482	4,026	115.6	-544	30,680	17,997	58.66	12,683	34,162	22,023	64.47	12,139
1976	3,765	3,954	105.0	-189	27,510	18,571	67.51	8,939	31,275	22,525	72.02	8,750
1977	4,122	3,893	94.4	229	25,826	19,076	73.86	6,750	30,037	22,969	76.47	7,068

1. Estimates differ from those in Exhibit 3.1 due to the use of different data sources.

Source: J.C. Musgrave, BEA, special tabulation.

Source: United States Department of Commerce, *A Study of Public Works Investment in the United States*, Washington, D.C., 1980 p. I-63.

5

Table 2
Comparative Public Facilities Condition Rating for Each Functional Area by City, January-February 1979

Condition Rating	Functional Category				
	Water System	Sewer System	Streets	Bridges	Mass Transit[1]
Poor and Deteriorating Rapidly				N, P	
Poor		N (collection)			SL
Poor-Fair, But Worsening			H, NO	H	
Poor-Fair			B, N, P, SL	B, NO, SL	
Poor-Fair, But Worsening		N (treatment)			NO
Fair, But Worsening	SL		S		
Fair	N (city)	SL		S	D
Fair, But Improving					DM, H, S
Fair-Good	B, NO, N (regional)	B, P (collection)	D		P
Good	D, H, P, S	D, DM, H, NO, S (treatment), S (collection)	DM	D	B
Good-Very Good		P (treatment)			
Very Good	DM			DM	

Note: B – Baltimore; D – Dallas; DM – Des Moines; H – Hartford; N – Newark; NO – New Orleans; P – Pittsburgh; SL – St. Louis; and S – Seattle.

1. Data on Newark's privately owned bus system were unavailable. Its condition rating is therefore omitted.

Source: Consad Corporation, *A Study of Public Works in the United States*, U.S. Department of Commerce, Washington, D.C., 1980.

2. The condition of streets in each of the surveyed cities (including fast-growing Dallas) was found to be poor.

3. The bridges in Pittsburgh and Newark were found to be deteriorating badly, and those of Baltimore, Hartford, New Orleans, and St. Louis to be in need of major repair.

Despite unmistakable evidence of such deterioration, the nation's public works investments, measured in constant dollars, fell from $38.6 billion in 1965 to less than $31 billion in 1977—a 21 percent decline. On a per capita basis, public works investments in constant dollars dropped from $198 per person in 1965 to $140 in 1977—a 29 percent decline. When measured against the value of the nation's Gross National Product, public works investments declined from 4.1 percent in 1965 to 2.3 percent in 1977—a 44 percent decline (Table 3). Each of these measures reflects that, although government expenditures have significantly increased during this same period, federal investments in public facilities have been declining both relatively and absolutely.

Part of the decline can be explained by reduced investment in the nation's highway system as the Interstate network nears completion and in education facilities, as the period of increased enrollment ends. Nonetheless, there has been a marked long-term decline in public works investments, even when highways and education are excluded. Moreover, even when investments associated with the assumption of responsibility for some public works by the private sector are included, there still has been an absolute decline in the percentage of GNP committed to capital investment in the nation's public facilities.[13]

The decline in public works investments has touched virtually every public works activity. As measured in non-inflationary 1972 purchasing power, during the period 1965-1978 there was more than a 50 percent drop in highway and street construction (Table 4). Conservation and development investments declined over 12 percent. Investments for improved water supply facilities also declined—even though the population substantially increased and water quality standards have become more rigid. The few areas of real growth in public works investments were in hospital construction, industrial facilities, and sewer systems. In each of these categories actual growth has been modest.

There are several reasons for these declines—a decrease in the nation's birth rate and the maturation of the "baby boom" have helped reduce the need for some kinds of investments. But the greater part of the decline reflects the growing habit of government at all levels to cut back on construction, rehabilitation, and maintenance in order to balance budgets, hold down the rate of tax growth, and finance a growing menu of social services. While such approaches keep budgets in balance and meet near-term needs, they impose serious long-term costs. Public facilities wear out and become obsolete.

Well-conceived public works are not a "pork barrel." This is a

7

Table 3
Public Works Investment in the United States
1965-1978
(1972 Constant Dollars)

Category	1965	1970	1971	1972	1973	1974	1975	1976	1977
Gross National Product (billions)	926	1,075		1,171	1,235	1,218	1,202	1,271	1,333
Population (millions)	194	204	207	209	210	211	213	215	217
Total Gross Capital Investment All Units of Government (billions)	38.6	37.5	36.9	35.9	36.2	36.8	34.8	32.0	30.4
Federal Investment	7.0	3.7	3.8	3.8	3.8	3.8	3.9	3.9	4.3
State and Local Investment	31.6	33.8	33.2	32.2	32.4	33.0	30.9	28.2	26.1
Public Works as a Percent of GNP	4.1	3.4		3.0	2.9	3.0	2.9	2.5	2.3
Per Capita Public Works Investment ($)	198	183	178	172	172	173	163	148	140

Source: Calculated from data found in the *Statistical Abstract of the United States, 1979*: Bureau of the Census, (100 edition). Washington, D.C., 1979: Table 479, p. 288; Table 715, p. 437; and Table 2, p. 6.

Table 4
Value of New Construction Put into Place
1965–1978
(Constant 1972 Dollars, millions)

Item	1965	1970	1975	1978
Total new construction	109,678	107,009	97,229	117,358
Private sector construction	75,948	75,113	68,628	91,189
Percent of total	69	70	71	78
Public sector construction	33,730	31,896	28,601	26,169
Percent of total	31	30	29	22
Buildings	12,245	12,008	11,207	9,151
Educational	6,693	6,336	5,607	3,779
Hospital	813	947	1,216	1,106
Industrial	576	561	663	718
Housing, redevelopment	856	1,239	572	578
Other public buildings	3,307	2,925	3,104	2,970
Highways and streets	11,651	11,282	7,269	5,685
Conservation, development	2,956	2,160	2,286	2,589
Military facilities	1,272	817	992	862
Other	5,606	5,629	6,847	7,883
Sewer systems	1,871	1,872	3,369	3,849
Water supply facilities	1,767	1,270	1,187	1,508
Miscellaneous	1,968	2,487	2,292	2,526

Source: U.S. Bureau of the Census, *Statistical Abstract of the United States: 1979,* (100 edition), Washington, D.C., 1979, page 774.

too-glib label attached to many investments that are essential. Deteriorating public facilities reduce the quality of life of virtually every American by diminishing essential community services. Investment in public works is as essential for national and local economic renewal as investment in our industrial plant itself. Indeed, economic development is dependent upon a sound public infrastructure.

FOOTNOTES TO CHAPTER 1

1. Federal Highway Administration, United States Department of Transportation, "1981 Federal Highway Legislation: Program and Revenue Options," Washington, D.C., June 26, 1980, pp. 2–3.

2. United States Department of Transportation, "Draft Transportation Agenda for the 1980s: The Issues," Washington, D.C., March 25, 1980, p. 15.

3. "1981 Federal Highway Legislation: Program and Revenue Options," pp. 3–9.

4. "1981 Federal Highway Legislation: Program and Revenue Options," p. 43.

5. General Accounting Office, *Additional Federal Aid for Urban Water Distribution Systems Should Wait Until Needs are Clearly Established,* Washington, D.C., November 24, 1980, p. 40.

6. United States Environmental Protection Agency, *The Cost of Clean Air and Water Report to Congress,* Washington, D.C., August, 1979, p. vii.

7. Goldin, Harrison J., *Deteriorating Infrastructure in Urban and Rural Areas,* Subcommittee on Economic Growth and Stabilization, Joint Economic Committee, Congress of the United States, Ninety-Sixth Congress, First Session, U.S. Government Printing Office, Washington, D.C., 1979, pp. 42–53.

8. Humphrey, Nancy; Peterson George E; Wilson, Peter, *The Future of Cleveland's Capital Plant,* The Urban Institute, Washington, D.C., 1979, pp. 52–73.

9. Wilson, Peter, *The Future of Dallas's Capital Plant,* The Urban Institute, Washington, D.C., 1980, pp. 27–40.

10. Business Week, "New Jails: Boom for Builders, Bust for Budgets," McGraw-Hill, February 9, 1981.

11. Choate, Pat, *The High Plains Project,* Economic Development Administration, United States Department of Commerce, Washington, D.C., 1978, pp. 1–3.

12. General Accounting Office, *Ways to Resolve Critical Water Resources Issues Facing the Nation,* Washington, D.C., April 27, 1979, pp. 23–25.

13. United States Department of Commerce, *A Study of Public Works Investment in the United States,* Washington, D.C., April, 1980, p. 19.

2

PUBLIC WORKS AND THE ECONOMY

Public works play a crucial role in the creation of national wealth and productivity growth. Education, research and development, and public works are the only real supply side *investments* the public sector makes in our economy.

Together with an aging industrial plant, deterioration of our public infrastructure has contributed to the decline in American productivity. Our *rate* of productivity improvement has fallen for almost 15 years and *absolute* levels of productivity have declined since 1979.[1] As national productivity weakens, so, too, does the nation's ability to finance private consumption, additional private capital investment and a diverse array of necessary governmental expenditures.

A number of recent studies suggests that these productivity reversals are the cumulative effect of: (1) a slowing rate of technological innovation and utilization; (2) inadequate rates of improvement in labor productivity; and (3) inadequate capital investment by both the public and private sectors in new and existing plants.[2] Attention has focused on technological decline, the quality of labor, and inadequate private capital investment. The role of public works in national development recently has been virtually ignored and dangerously regarded as the "pork barrel." While some public works have been misguided and can be labeled as "pork," it is both unwise and dangerous to castigate all public works as falling into that category.

A primary objective of public works investment is to provide basic public services, such as water supplies, waste water treatment, and transportation that underpin the operation of the national and local economies. Simultaneously, $80 billion in annual public works investments can also be used to:

■ assist in national economic stabilization (achieving a desired level of employment, output, income, and prices);

■ assist in stabilizing state and local budgets; and

■ assist specific geographic areas, economic sectors or population groups, in eliminating the problems of economic obsolescence.

PUBLIC WORKS AND JOBS

The construction industry is a major sector in the U.S. economy. In 1977, over 477,000 firms were directly engaged in construction activity. They employed over 4.2 million persons in a variety of activities and trades, of which some 3.5 million were construction workers (Table 5). These workers earned in excess of $43 billion.

Public works investments account for a substantial share of construction activity. Of the $223 billion in new construction put in place in 1980, over $56.7 billion was public works—more than 24 percent of the total investment (Table 6). Furthermore, the public sector invested an additional $30 billion in the purchase of right-of-ways, existing buildings, and equipment.[3]

Table 5
Firms and Employment in the Construction Industry
1977

Contract Construction	472.5	4,212	3,542
General Building Contractors	133.1	1,150	938
Heavy Construction Contractors	28.0	827	709
Special Trade Contractors	288.6	2,158	1,846
Plumbing, Heating, and Air Conditioning	56.5	458	368
Painting, Paperhanging, and Decorating	27.3	133	121
Electrical Work	36.8	366	305
Masonry and Stonework	24.8	152	143
Plastering, Drywall and Insulation	16.8	186	164
Terrazzo, Tile, Marble, and Mosaic Work	3.9	22	19
Carpentering	24.3	124	114
Floor Laying and Floor Work	9.0	41	34
Roofing and Sheet Metal	20.6	172	146
Concrete Work	18.4	139	125
Water Well Drilling	4.3	22	19
Structural Steel Erection	2.6	48	41
Glass and Glazing Work	3.2	24	18
Excavating and Foundation Work	16.2	103	91
Wrecking and Demolition Work	1.0	9	7
Subdividers and Developers	5.3	43	19
TOTAL	477.8	4,254	3,561

Source: U.S. Bureau of the Census, *Statistical Abstract of the United States: 1979,* (100 edition), Washington, D.C., 1970, page 776.

Table 6
New Construction Put in Place: Trends and Projections 1978–81
(in millions of current dollars)

Type of construction	1978	1979	1980¹	Percent change 1979–80	1981*	Percent change 1980–81
Total new construction	205,457	228,950	228,300	0	270,330	18
Private construction	159,556	179,948	171,600	-5	206,700	20
Residential buildings	93,424	99,030	84,000	-15	109,800	31
New housing units	75,808	78,587	60,800	-23	83,000	37
Additions and alterations	16,349	18,236	20,000	11	23,000	15
Nonhousekeeping	1,267	2,206	3,200	45	3,800	20
Nonresidential buildings	36,293	47,298	53,100	12	60,700	14
Industrial	10,994	14,950	13,800	-8	15,200	10
Office	6,574	9,461	13,200	40	17,200	30
Other commercial	11,991	15,463	17,800	15	19,600	10
Religious	1,248	1,548	1,600	5	1,700	5
Educational	729	806	1,200	50	1,300	10
Hospital and institutional	3,347	3,530	3,500	0	3,500	0
Miscellaneous	1,410	1,540	2,000	30	2,200	10
Farm, nonresidential	5,253	5,700	5,700	0	5,700	0
Public utilities	23,302	26,467	27,300	3	28,900	6
Telephone	5,418	6,343	7,300	15	8,400	15
Electric light and power	14,384	16,009	15,200	-5	13,700	-10
Gas	1,929	2,266	2,700	20	4,300	60

Table 6 (Continued)
New Construction Put in Place: Trends and Projections 1978–81
(in millions of current dollars)

Type of construction	1978	1979	1980[1]	Percent change 1979–80	1981[1]	Percent change 1980–81
Railroad	1,037	1,259	1,500	20	1,800	20
Petroleum pipelines	534	591	600	0	700	10
All other private	1,283	1,452	1,500	0	1,600	10
Public construction	45,902	49,003	56,700	16	63,600	12
Buildings	15,241	15,857	18,100	14	20,100	11
Housing and redevelopment	1,051	1,211	1,600	35	2,000	28
Industrial	1,184	1,411	1,800	30	2,300	30
Educational	6,264	6,903	7,700	12	8,500	10
Hospital	1,822	1,648	1,600	0	1,600	0
Other public	4,919	4,684	5,400	15	5,700	5
Highways and streets	10,712	11,915	15,500	30	17,800	15
Military facilities	1,512	1,640	1,700	5	2,000	20
Conservation and development	4,457	4,587	5,000	10	5,500	10
Other public construction	13,989	15,003	16,400	9	18,200	11
Sewer systems	6,765	7,298	7,700	5	8,500	10
Water supply facilities	2,661	2,490	3,500	40	4,200	20
Miscellaneous	4,563	5,215	5,200	0	5,500	5

1. Estimated by Bureau of Industrial Economics.

Source: United States Department of Commerce, *1981 U.S. Industrial Outlook*, Washington, D.C., 1981, p. 6.

Source: Bureau of the Census and Bureau of Industrial Economics.

14

The construction industry and the public works component of that industry extends far beyond the 4.25 million persons employed in direct construction activities. It is closely linked with a set of industry and service institutions, each of which feels the effects when the construction industry declines (Table 7). The Rand Corporation and U.S. Department of Labor traced these industrial linkages for 22 types of public works projects. For each type of project, the distribution of funds was followed to final destination (either direct on-site construction labor or the acquisition of specific materials and equipment) (Tables 8 and 9). The conclusions drawn from this analysis are:

■ The most significant short-term impacts of public works projects are found in equipment, material and other industries rather than in on-site construction. For every direct on-site construction job created by public works projects, three additional jobs are created in the overall economy.

■ There are substantial variations in the number of on-site construction jobs created by various types of public works projects. Public school construction requires almost 25 percent less on-site labor than college housing construction. Highway construction uses less than one-half as much on-site labor as that of dam, levee and local flood control projects.

■ Substantial variations exist in the quantities and types of materials and equipment used in public works projects.

Such variations are important because we can take advantage of them to tailor public works investments to meet a number of objectives including stabilization of the economy, alleviation of structural unemployment, and helping places suffering from economic obsolescence to adapt to new economic development possibilities.

PUBLIC WORKS AND PLACES

A large and growing number of communities are now hamstrung in their economic revitalization efforts because their basic public facilities—their streets, roads, water systems, and sewerage treatment plants—are either too limited, obsolete, or worn out to sustain a modernized industrial economy. As a rule of thumb, when a community wastewater treatment system is operating at 80 percent of capacity, that community will not be able to add additional industrial load. This is particularly true for smaller communities where the 20 percent of excess capacity will, in actual quantitative terms, represent limited treatment abilities. The operating ratio for water treatment that indicates effective full capacity utilization is 70 percent. A Department of Commerce survey of 6,870 communities' wastewater treatment capacity reports that 3,133 (46%) of these systems are operating at 80 percent of capacity or higher. The same survey indicates that 1,844 of 5,622 places have water treatment systems operating at 70 percent or greater capacity. When deficient transportation,

Table 7
Distribution of Inputs and Outputs:
New Construction Industries
(SIC CODES: PARTS 1112, 1212, 148, 15–17)

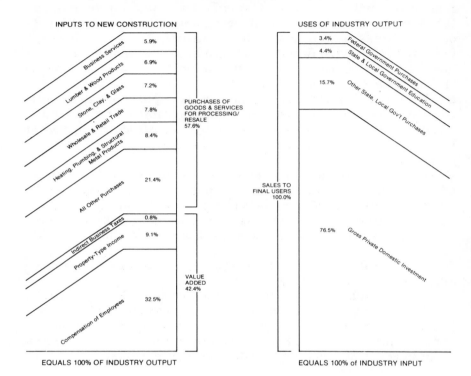

The new construction industry requires a high proportion of manufactured goods and services supplied by other industries (intermediate products) as inputs. As these flow through the construction process, value is added by the capital and labor employed to produce the industry output—buildings, highways, dams, etc.

Value added by construction labor and capital in the processing and resale of these inputs accounts for the remaining industry costs, with compensation of employees the largest component, as is the case for most industries.

The output of this industry is classified as fixed investment and all of it goes to final users such as purchasers of new housing, industrial plant and other business structures. The private sector takes three-fourths, and Governments—Federal, state and local— take about one-fourth of the total output.

Note: Percent distributions are based on the 1972 Input-Output table; shipments are valued at producer prices.

Source: U.S. Department of Commerce, *U.S. Industrial Outlook, 1980,* Washington, D.C., 1980.

publicly operated solid waste and toxic waste disposal sites, and other public facilities essential to private sector investment are also considered, at least one half (and more likely two-thirds) of the nation's communities are unable to support modernized development *until* major new investments are made in their basic facilities that undergird the economy.

A number of studies have attempted to measure the influence of public works on the location and investment decisions of individual firms. The most comprehensive was conducted in the mid-1970s by the Bureau of Census.[5] Over 2,000 firms operating in 254 distinct product classes were examined. Each firm was asked whether the availability of certain public works facilities were either: (1) critical; (2) significant; or (3) of minimal value in their location decisions. The survey indicated that for virtually all of the 254 categories studied, the availability of public works facilities was of either critical or significant importance to location decisions. The availability of public facilities was almost always a more important locational consideration than the existence of local tax incentives or local industrial revenue bond financing. Indeed, while public works in themselves are never a sufficient condition for economic development, they are almost always a necessary condition.

PUBLIC WORKS AND ECONOMIC STABILIZATION

It has long been a standing assumption that public works investments can be modulated to help stabilize the ups and downs of the economy. However, in practice, the U.S. has given little attention to such uses of annual public works expenditures.

The present recession is the sixth such decline in the economy since the end of World War II. As with previous recessions, the 1980–81 economic decline has created substantial unemployment and under-utilization of production capacities in the construction, materials, and equipment industries. The national unemployment rate in the construction industry averaged 17 percent in 1980; it rose as high as 40 percent in some regions. The steel industry, heavily related to construction, operated at approximately 50 percent of its capacity throughout 1980, creating 80,000 unemployed steel workers.

Economic policy might reduce the impact of such a severe recession by using the nation's annual $80 billion public works investments as a counter-cyclical economic tool for providing employment in the construction, materials and equipment industries. However, public works investments in the United States have long been made in a perverse pro-cyclical pattern, increasing during the expansionary phase of economic cycle and decreasing during its contractionary phase. This pro-cyclical management of public works investments creates many adverse consequences:

Table 8
Construction Costs, by Type of Building Construction, Allocated for Industrial Sectors and On-Site Labor
(in dollars per $1000 of total contract cost, 1974)

SIC	Description	Private One-Family Housing	Public Housing	Schools	Hospitals	Nursing Homes	College Housing	Federal Office Buildings
14	Mining, non-metallic metals, except fuel	2.60	—	—	—	—	—	—
22	Textile mill products	3.70	—	—	—	—	—	—
26	Paper and allied products	1.70	—	—	.40	2.20	.80	#
28	Chemicals and allied products	4.20	4.60	2.50	3.20	3.70	2.40	1.70
29	Petroleum products	4.60	5.70	6.60	2.30	5.10	2.50	2.00
30	Rubber and misc. plastic products	3.80	—	—	.30	.40	#	#
	Total Non-durable Goods Manufacturing	18.00	10.30	9.10	6.10	11.40	5.70	3.70
24	Lumber and wood products	117.50	40.20	33.50	16.00	30.50	33.20	9.10
25	Furniture and fixtures	.20	.60	7.70	1.00	.60	.70	.70
32	Stone, clay, and glass products	44.20	47.90	60.90	47.60	56.90	50.40	38.90
33	Primary metal products	14.40	15.90	7.20	15.80	10.70	7.10	10.40
34	Fabricated metal products	26.70	68.20	83.90	77.90	81.70	77.90	60.00
35	Machinery, except electrical (and excluding construction machinery)	4.20	6.40	8.60	30.70	21.30	7.80	31.70
	Construction equipment[a]	5.40	13.90	13.60	11.80	10.10	12.50	15.20
36	Electrical equipment and supplies	14.70	21.90	24.80	37.00	26.00	19.40	30.00
37	Transportation equipment[a]	2.40	NA	NA	NA	NA	NA	NA
38	Instruments and related products	.20	#	4.30	5.70	3.60	1.30	3.40
	Total Durable Goods Manufacturing	233.70	222.10	251.40	245.60	243.00	211.70	200.70

Row							
Other Materials not otherwise classified[b]	3.80	7.10	7.00	2.10	1.60	1.50	1.30
Transportation	11.20	7.50	9.40	8.00	8.80	11.60	9.00
Wholesale and retail trade	183.20	184.10	255.60	238.20	240.60	271.00	280.30
Total Material, Equipment and Supply Cost	448.80	424.00	525.50	497.90	503.80	500.00	493.60
Total On-Site Labor Cost	214.60	359.40	303.60	338.20	332.70[c]	377.40	374.40
Total Unallocated Cost[d]	336.50	216.60	170.80	163.90	163.60[c]	122.60	131.80
Total Project Cost	1000.00	1000.00	1000.00	1000.00	1000.00	1000.00	1000.00
Ratio of total on-site labor cost to total project cost	.21	.36	.30	.34	.33	.38	.37
Ratio of total on-site labor cost to total cost of materials, equipment, and supplies	.48	.85	.58	.68	.66	.75	.76

SOURCES: Ball, Claiborne M, "Employment Effects of Construction Expenditures," *Monthly Labor Review*, February 1965, pp. 154–158; *Labor and Material Requirements for College Housing Construction*, BLS Bulletin 1441, May 1965, pp. 7, 28–31; *Labor and Material Requirements for Construction of Private Single-Family Houses*, BLS Bulletin 1755, 1972, p. 9, 17–20; *Labor and Material Requirements for Hospital and Nursing Home Construction*, BLS Bulletin 1691, 1971, pp. 11, 39–42, 48–50; *Labor and Material Requirements for Public Housing Construction*, BLS Bulletin 1821, 1974, pp. 8–10; *Labor and Material Requirements for School Construction*, BLS Bulletin 1588, June 1968, pp. 6, 19–21.

NOTES: NA means not available. — = not applicable. # means less than $.20 and more than zero. Columns may not add to total because of rounding. Data in the table are expressed in 1974 dollars. The year of survey for each type of project is as follows: private one-family housing—1969, public housing—1973, schools—1965, hospitals and nursing homes—1966, college housing—1961, and federal office buildings—1959.

[a] Where no separate data were available for the cost of transportation equipment, this cost has been included in the cost of construction equipment. The data under both categories are rental costs—i.e., the cost of owning (depreciation) and maintaining the equipment.

[b] Includes nursery products and materials not itemized by the contractors.

[c] On-site labor and unallocated costs for nursing homes have been estimated using data for hospitals.

[d] Includes warehousing, some off-site salaries, supplemental wage benefits, administration and clerical work, expenses of the central office, and yard operations.

Table 9

Construction Costs by Types of Heavy Construction Allocated to Industrial Sectors and On-Site Labor

(in dollars per $1000 of total contract cost, 1974)

SIC	Description	Highways	Sewer Works — Lines	Sewer Works — Plants	Large Earth Fill Dams	Small Earth Fill Dams	Local Flood Protection	Pile Dikes	Levees	Revetments	Powerhouse Construction	Medium Concrete Dams	Lock and Concrete Dams	Large Multiple Purpose Projects	Dredging	Misc.[a]
14	Mining, nonmetallic metals, except fuel[b]	—	—	—	#	15.00	25.10	77.30	45.30	208.70	6.10	1.20	42.50	24.80	#	14.70
22	Textile mill products	NA	—	—	NA	NA	NA	NA	NA	NA	NA	NA	NA	NA	NA	NA
26	Paper and allied products		—	—	NA	NA	NA	NA	NA	NA	NA	NA	NA	NA	NA	NA
28	Chemicals and allied products	2.80	.90	2.40	NA	NA	NA	NA	NA	NA	NA	NA	NA	NA	NA	NA
29	Petroleum products	59.10	8.30	5.20	NA	NA	NA	NA	NA	NA	NA	NA	NA	NA	NA	NA
30	Rubber and misc. plastic products		—	—	NA	NA	NA	NA	NA	NA	NA	NA	NA	NA	NA	NA
	Total Non-durable Goods Manufacturing	61.90	9.20	7.60	65.60	77.80	23.70	33.00	61.90	34.30	5.90	13.70	14.30	17.50	72.60	85.80
24	Lumber and wood products[c]	5.30	2.70	5.70	6.80	5.10	9.90	46.90	.80	42.60	12.20	4.20	4.30	4.90	#	17.20
25	Furniture and fixtures	—	—	—	NA	NA	NA	NA	NA	NA	NA	NA	NA	NA	NA	NA
32	Stone, clay and glass products	79.30	123.30	39.60	9.30	6.60	44.20	—	.70	#	11.10	60.70	80.90	38.10	—	36.20
33	Primary metal products	NA	27.00	37.00	1.80	3.50	4.30	3.60	.90	3.90	13.90	28.70	60.90	30.00	40.40	32.50
34	Fabricated metal products	67.70	6.70	47.10	39.40	21.70	85.90	11.30	6.90	6.90	34.70	57.10	37.30	52.00	14.90	3.60
35	Machinery, except electrical (and excluding construction machinery)	—	6.50	60.90	11.40	10.60	2.20	5.30	.80	#	232.70	34.10	44.10	31.30	.80	7.70
	Construction equipment[d]	83.60[e]	95.80	69.00	83.40	120.20	31.90	48.30	56.80	16.60	23.10	65.80	89.10	33.90	25.90	87.00
36	Electrical equipment and supplies	—	1.10	16.10	.90	.90	.40	—	#	—	153.20	1.30	8.40	19.20	#	#
37	Transportation equipment[d]	NA	NA	NA	43.40	41.90	11.50	26.60	12.70	12.30	2.70	11.60	12.10	3.20	85.70	28.50
38	Instruments and related products[f]	—	—	3.00	NA	NA	NA	—	NA	—	NA	NA	—	NA	NA	NA
	Total Durable Goods Manufacturing	301.60	264.10	281.10	196.30	211.10	190.30	142.00	79.50	82.20	486.30	263.40	337.20	213.90	167.70	213.40
	Other materials, not elsewhere classified[g]	65.80	1.10	2.70	#	.70	#	—	#	—	2.50	#	—	1.30	#	.70
	Transportation[h]	6.60	9.00	7.00	19.10	36.80	44.00	105.50	63.40	251.50	31.60	22.20	74.30	44.70	20.50	42.40
	Wholesale and retail trade	177.20	252.60	246.20	149.20	149.30	103.00	89.80	71.40	103.30	140.30	106.40	130.90	75.90	73.20	139.30

Type of Heavy Construction — Civil Works

20

Total material, equipment and supply cost	547.40	534.90	542.00	430.00	490.00	386.10	447.70	321.60	679.90	670.10	406.90	599.20	376.90	334.00	495.70
Total on-site labor cost[i]	226.00	304.80	330.80	434.00	441.80	510.70	416.10	494.90	192.60	297.50	486.30	368.70	555.20	511.70	391.90
Total unallocated cost[j]	226.60	160.30	127.10	132.80	68.10	103.20	136.20	183.60	127.30	32.40	106.90	32.00	67.90	154.40	112.40
Total project cost	1000.00	1000.00	1000.00	1000.00	1000.00	1000.00	1000.00	1000.00	1000.00	1000.00	1000.00	1000.00	1000.00	1000.00	1000.00
Ratio of total on-site labor costs to total project cost	.23	.30	.33	.43	.44	.51	.42	.49	.19	.30	.49	.37	.56	.51	.39
Ratio of total on-site labor costs to total cost of materials, equipment and supplies	.41	.57	.61	1.00	.90	1.32	.93	1.54	.28	.44	1.20	.62	1.47	1.53	.79

SOURCES: Claiborne M. Bell, "Employment Effects of Construction Expenditures," *Monthly Labor Review*, February 1965, pp. 154–158: Robert Ball, "Labor and Materials Required for Highway Construction," *Monthly Labor Review*, June 1973, pp. 40–45: Diane S. Finger, "Labor Requirements for Federal Highway Construction," *Monthly Labor Review*, December 1975, pp. 31–36; Robert H. Haveman and John V. Krutilla, *Unemployment, Idle Capacity, and the Evaluation of Public Expenditures: National and Regional Analyses*, Johns Hopkins Press, Baltimore, 1968, pp. 20–21; *Labor and Material Requirements for Construction of Federally Aided Highways, 1958, 1961 and 1964*, BLS Report 299, p. 5; *Labor and Material Requirements for Sewer Works Construction, 1968*, BLS Bulletin 1490, pp. 6, 24–25.

NOTES: NA means not available. — = not applicable. # means less than $.20 and more than zero. Columns may not add up to total because of rounding. Data in the table are expressed in 1974 dollars. The year of survey for each type of project is as follows: highways—1963; sewer works—1963; and civil works—1960. (The data for civil works have been inflated from 1958 prices.)

a. Miscellaneous includes four projects not elsewhere classified under the Civil Works heading: Bayou Macon Channel Improvement (Louisiana): Jetties, Gold Beach (Oregon): Outlet Channel, Sardis Dam (Mississippi); and Sea Wall Extension, Galveston (Texas).

b. The data given for civil works projects include metal, coal, and crude petroleum mining.

c. The cost of lumber products includes the cost of furniture and fixtures: (SIC 25) for all civil work projects. However, very little is spent on furniture and fixtures in the construction of civil works projects.

d. Where no data are given for the cost of transportation equipment, it has been included in the cost of construction equipment. The data under both categories are rental costs—i.e., the cost of owning (depreciation) and maintaining the equipment.

e. The cost of construction equipment for highways has been estimated from data for similar projects completed in an earlier year.

f. For civil works projects, SIC 38 is included in "Other Materials, not elsewhere classified."

g. Includes nursery products and, except for civil works projects, materials not itemized by the contractors. For civil works projects, this category also includes SIC 38, Instruments and Related Products, and SIC 39, Miscellaneous Manufacturing. For highways, it also includes some paints and other chemicals, aluminum, and paper products.

h. In the data for civil works projects, transportation costs include warehousing. For all other projects, warehousing is included in unallocated costs.

i. Estimates of costs for contractor-employed inspectors and engineers are included in on-site labor costs for civil works projects. For all other projects, these costs are included in the "Total Unallocated Cost" category.

j. For civil works projects, include contractor's tax payments, earnings from payments for rents and interest, corporate profits after taxes, overhead (including mobilization and demobilization costs), and services. For all other types of projects it includes, in addition, warehousing, some off-site salaries, supplemental wage benefits, administration and clerical work, expenses of the central office, and yard operations.

Table 10
Municipal and Industrial Wastewater and Water Treatment by Capacities by State

State	Wastewater Treatment			Water Treatment		
	Number of Places Surveyed	Number of Places Using 80 Percent or More of Capacity	Percent of Total Surveyed	Number of Places Surveyed	Number of Places Using 70 Percent or More of Capacity	Percent of Total Surveyed
Alabama	156	63	40.3	121	54	44.6
Alaska	11	6	54.5	22	10	45.4
Arizona	62	29	46.7	18	5	27.7
Arkansas	112	57	50.8	75	15	20.0
California	369	229	62.0	271	70	25.8
Colorado	95	45	47.3	80	5	6.2
Connecticut	90	34	37.7	56	18	32.1
Delaware	11	3	27.2	19	8	42.1
Florida	231	85	36.7	177	54	30.5
Georgia	215	83	38.6	132	55	41.6
Hawaii	29	6	20.6	3	1	33.3
Idaho	41	18	43.9	27	10	37.0
Illinois	363	188	51.7	386	177	45.8
Indiana	133	72	54.1	176	85	48.2
Iowa	124	60	48.3	129	35	27.1
Kansas	144	66	45.8	104	15	14.4
Kentucky	114	55	48.2	122	72	59.0
Louisiana	155	66	42.5	157	49	31.2
Maine	57	29	50.8	81	30	37.0
Maryland	76	22	28.9	50	N/A	N/A
Massachusetts	92	30	32.6	200	48	24.0
Michigan	203	N/A	N/A	165	21	12.7
Minnesota	117	42	35.8	168	15	8.9
Mississippi	96	25	26.0	129	67	51.9
Missouri	186	71	38.1	124	43	34.6
Montana	39	19	48.7	16	5	31.2
Nebraska	59	28	47.4	56	8	14.2
Nevada	22	8	36.3	15	3	20.0
New Hampshire	33	17	51.5	55	15	27.2
New Jersey	242	126	52.0	218	101	46.3
New Mexico	45	15	33.3	31	5	16.1

Table 10 (Continued)
Municipal and Industrial Wastewater and Water Treatment by Capacities by State

State	Wastewater Treatment			Water Treatment		
	Number of Places Surveyed	Number of Places Using 80 Percent or More of Capacity	Percent of Total Surveyed	Number of Places Surveyed	Number of Places Using 70 Percent or More of Capacity	Percent of Total Surveyed
New York	363	187	51.5	N/A	N/A	N/A
North Carolina	163	73	44.7	240	21	8.7
North Dakota	23	11	47.8	N/A	N/A	N/A
Ohio	400	212	53.0	498	276	55.4
Oklahoma	166	65	39.1	157	17	10.8
Oregon	96	20	20.8	158	18	11.3
Pennsylvania	461	198	42.9	288	177	61.4
Rhode Island	14	4	28.5	18	4	22.2
South Carolina	202	105	51.9	120	30	25.0
South Dakota	27	16	59.2	31	2	6.4
Tennessee	136	56	41.1	113	30	26.5
Texas	486	285	58.6	121	57	47.1
Utah	48	30	62.5	38	5	13.1
Vermont	45	25	55.5	33	15	45.4
Virginia	137	65	47.4	122	43	35.2
Washington	102	36	35.2	113	6	5.3
West Virginia	77	39	50.6	110	37	33.6
Wisconsin	176	101	57.3	60	2	3.3
Wyoming	26	8	30.7	19	5	26.3
TOTAL	6,870	3,133	45.6 (46.9)[2]	5,622	1,844	32.7 (33.0)[2]

Source: Reid, George; Martin, Ralph; and Pulliam, J. Gordon, University of Oklahoma and Pulliam Associates under contract to the Economic Development Administration, United States Department of Commerce. *Report on Municipal and Industrial Wastewater Treatment Systems: A Statistical Compendium*, June 1978, and *Report on Municipal and Industrial Water Treatment Systems: A Statistical Compendium*, January 1978, Norman, Oklahoma, 1978.

1. As a rule of thumb, when a community wastewater treatment system is operating at 80 percent of capacity, that community will not be able to add additional industrial load. This is particularly true for smaller communities where the 20 percent of excess capacity will in actual quantitative terms represent limited treatment abilities. The operating ratio for water treatment that indicates effective full capacity utilization is 70 percent.

2. Excludes the N.A. (not available) states in the computation of percentages. Otherwise, the totals reflect percentage of those actually reported communities.

23

■ By increasing public works investments during the expansionary phase of the economic cycle, costs (materials, equipment, and labor) become artificially high and contribute to inflation; and

■ By decreasing public works investments during the contractionary phases, under-utilization of labor and industrial facilities increase in the construction, materials and equipment industries—worsening the recession.

Since 1960 Congress has enacted three public works counter-cyclical programs—the $1.9 billion Accelerated Public Works Program, (APW) in 1961-1962; the $130 million Public Works Impact Program (PWIP) in 1972-1973; and the $6 billion Local Public Works Impact Program (LPW) in 1976-1977. A number of studies have concluded that the three temporary programs fell far short of meeting their *stated* objectives, i.e., stimulating employment for the structurally-unemployed in distressed areas during an economic downturn. Evidence suggests that these shortcomings lay in the timing and administration of these expenditures and in the narrowness of the goals of the program.[6]

The temporary counter-cyclical Local Public Works program of 1976-1977 did nothing to relieve the 1974-1977 recession until late 1976. Over 80 percent of the direct employment generated by the LPW projects did not occur until the recovery phase of the cycle had begun. These time lags reflect less on the efficacy of public works as a counter-cyclical device than they do on the sclerosis of the executive and legislative process. Lags occurred because of delays in securing passage of legislation, Presidential approval, appropriation of funds, selection of projects, and construction. Two years after the onset of the 1974 recession, the Ford Administration continued to resist adding to the budget deficit by refusing to use counter-cyclical public works for economic stabilization, relying instead on traditional fiscal and monetary measures until the summer of 1976.

Occasional recessions are inevitable. The annual $35 billion federal public works expenditures can exert major economic stabilizing influences. Thus, it is both timely and prudent to devise policies and administrative techniques for managing public works investments in anticipation of the economic cycle.

A Permanent Counter-Cyclical Use of Public Works—If public works investments are to be used as a flywheel on the economy, we must make a choice between the relatively small-scale temporary programs of the past and a more permanent policy that governs the timing of investments of all federal public works programs. The federal government has a large array of permanent public works programs which could be used as a counter-cyclical tool. Several are directly federal, such as the public works construction of the Corps of Engineers. However, approximately 80 percent of the funds that the federal government invests in public works are in grants-in-aid to state and local governments.[7] Some of these federal funds are in the form of revenue sharing or by block grants such as the Community Development Block Grant Program (CDBG). Most are made available through categorical programs such as those of the Environmental Protection Agency, the Federal Highway Administration, the Farmers Home Administration, and the programs of the Economic Development Administration, among many others. Federal transfers of funds and direct investments constitute 50 percent of all financing of public works construction in the U.S. Much of the remaining 50 percent of construction financing represents matching grants by state and local governments to meet federal requirements or mandated federal investments.

There are many possible advantages to the use of these public works funds as a counter-cyclical tool. The first, and perhaps most important, is to reduce the adverse consequences created by the present pro-cyclical pattern of these investments. In many ways present pro-cyclical investment patterns for public works are akin to loose cargo in a ship in turbulent waters. As the ship sways side-to-side the cargo shifts and accentuates the sways. The counter-cyclical management would directly address this issue, something temporary programs cannot, by their very nature, accomplish.

A large portion of the benefits of counter-cyclical public works projects can be generated during the contractionary phase of the economy cycle if political and ideologically generated delays are eliminated. Also, economic recovery in the initial phases of the expansionary phases of the cycle can be accelerated. After all, there is little merit in having massive unemployment and unused production capacity in a slow recovery period. A number of reforms are worth discussion including (1) stand-by authorities; (2) the identification of a backlog of projects which would serve both counter-cyclical purposes and long-term national and local development; and (3) the creation of purchasing techniques which would permit stockpiling of materials and equipment for use in future projects.

A permanent, more systematic counter-cyclical policy for public works programs would also reduce the "crisis" management atmosphere which has existed in temporary programs, such as LPW, funded on a "crash" basis. Temporary funding created very strong political pressures when applicants realized the existence of a "now or never," one-time-only project funding opportunity. For example, in LPW there were over $22 billion of applications for $6 billion of funds. The crisis management approach of "get out the money," with quality often a secondary consideration, would also be obviated. In a permanent program, administrators would be able to better meet their responsibility to choose worthy projects. By advancing projects or adding projects to permanent programs, many of the political pressures created in temporary programs can be substantially reduced—

25

particularly the very intense pressure generated around marginal projects.

A third advantage to permanent programs would be a reduction in lags between the beginning of a recession and the time when benefits would begin to flow. Since the end of the Second World War the nation has gained substantial experience in economic policy. The tools of economic analysis have been substantially improved. The use of permanent programs would permit the acceleration of projects at a very early stage in the economic decline and would permit a timely reduction of effort as the economy moved to advanced recovery. The use of permanent programs would facilitate advance purchase programs for a wide array of equipment materials.

A fourth advantage to the adoption of a permanent, counter-cyclically administered public works policy would be to help ensure that federal funds are not used to replace state and local funds. In permanent programs, the source of local matching funds is generally mandated as a federal funding requisite. By advancing the pipeline, this fiscal integrity can be maintained. However, when it is desirable to waive matching requirements in order to aid state and local fiscal stability, such actions could be taken explicitly.

A fifth advantage would be to facilitate better targeted investments in order to address regional and sectoral variations in the economic cycle. Roger Vaughan has documented how regionally disparate these cycles often are. By the use of advance purchases in specific industries located in specific places, economic stimulus can be achieved. Conversely, in the expansionary phase of the cycle, purchases can be deferred or placed in specific sectors or places needing stimulus. Vaughan has also described how state stabilization funds could be created to finance such projects.[8]

A sixth advantage of a permanent counter-cyclical program would be the improved fiscal stability it could help bring to state and local public works expenditures. Public works constitute a significant component of most state and local budgets, averaging about 15 percent.[9] Public works funds are often cut back during a contractionary period, especially in major urban areas the fiscal base of which is already deteriorating. Forestalling state and local cutbacks in essential maintenance and rehabilitation through a counter-cyclical federal spending pattern would help state and local governments avoid even larger capital replacement investments in the future. And such a program could be more effectively targeted to help the unemployed as well.

Targeting—In the past, federal public works programs adopted to put the structurally unemployed back to work in economically distressed places yielded disappointing results.

Past experiences of the LPW and PWIP programs indicate that relatively little of the employment they created went to the long-term unemployed, the unskilled, or even to those persons living in places where individual projects were constructed. Indeed, construction wages constitute only a minor share (22 percent) of total public works expenditures. Vaughan and the Office of Management and Budget have analyzed the targeting of counter-cyclical public works to distressed areas and to structurally unemployed persons.[10] They conclude:

■ The majority of the expended funds for PWIP and LWP projects did *not* go to direct employment for on-site construction but rather to the related materials, equipment and associated industries;

■ Employment directly created by these projects did not greatly affect the unemployed. In the PWIP program, the unemployed accounted for only 27 percent of the total jobs generated and accounted for less than seven percent of the program budget. The LPW program employed even fewer. Only 12 percent of the jobs went to the unemployed, a total of two percent of the overall budget;

■ The duration of employment created for workers was short. Under the PWIP program, the average project employment period for unskilled workers was 3.7 weeks; for skilled workers it was only 4.2 weeks. Under the LPW program the average project period of employment for unskilled workers was 3.9 weeks; and for skilled workers 3.6 weeks. Since their experience tenure was brief, most unskilled workers did not receive adequate on-the-job training to prepare them for other employment.

Evaluations of the LPW and PWIP programs by the Economic Development Administration and the Office of Management and Budget also concluded that much of the on-site construction employment went to persons not residing in the area, many of them employees of construction firms located outside the area where the public works project was constructed.

However, by careful planning, government *can* target benefits to help both people and specific industries. Studies by the Rand Corporation concluded that in the recessions since the end of the Second World War, there has been excess capacity in the materials and equipment industries in the contractionary phases of the economic cycle. In this present cycle, the steel, aluminum, fabricated metals, concrete, equipment and related industries find themselves operating at substantially less than full capacity. To address this economic sluggishness, the present $100 billion backlog of funded, but unspent, public works funds could be used to purchase needed materials and equipment in advance of actual construction. This would produce many benefits. For example, purchasing steel at a time when that industry is operating at 54 percent of capacity would avoid ensuing price rises; permit the industry to operate closer to normal levels of production; improve conditions of certainty in that sector; create jobs for laid-off workers, many of whom reside in distressed areas; and eliminate almost $10 million per week in unemployment payments. Tables 8 and 9 identify the range of industries that could be similarly assisted.

Targeting specific sectors can be an effective means for addressing major regional variations that exist in the economic cycle. Pre-purchasing would also provide a stimulus to basic industries operating at low capacity with high unemployment in distressed places.

ECONOMIC STABILITY OUT OF PROGRAM CHAOS

In a decade of severe fiscal constraint, when we face the major necessities of economic revitalization, we cannot pursue the open-ended, excessively fragmented approaches to policy so typical of the past. Fiscal and economic austerity is the order of the day. The benefits of each dollar must be stretched as far as we can take them. We now face the need to shift from a purely legislatively-dominated approach to public works at the national level to one in which the Executive Branch provides a disciplined base of analysis and priorities designed to ensure public works expenditures that meet the long-term needs of national economic renewal in phase with the shorter-term needs of economic policy dictated by the rise and fall of the economic cycle. Such reforms are possible, will save money, and make the capital we have go further.

But how can we find the capital we need to meet all of the competing demands in the 1980s?

FOOTNOTES TO CHAPTER 2

1. Schwartz, Gail Garfield and Choate, Pat, *Being Number One: Rebuilding the U.S. Economy,* Lexington Books, Lexington, Massachusetts, 1980.

2. U.S. Bureau of Labor Statistics, *Productivity and the Economy,* Bulletin 1926, Washington, D.C., 1979.

3. *Statistical Abstract,* 1979, p. 288.

4. Vernez, George; Vaughan, Roger; Burright, Burke; and Coleman, Sinclair, *Regional Cycles and Employment Effects of Public Works Investments,* The Rand Corporation, Santa Monica, California, January, 1977, pp. v–xx.

5. United States Department of Commerce, *Industrial Location Determinants,* 1971–1975, Washington, D.C., 1973.

6. Sulvetta, Anthony, *Public Works as Countercyclical Assistance,* Office of Management and Budget, Executive Office of the President of the United States, Washington, D.C., November, 1979.

7. *A Study of Public Works Investment in the United States,* pp. 14–18.

8. Vaughan, Roger, *Public Works as a Countercyclical Tool,* Joint Economic Committee of the Congress of the United States, September, 1980.

9. *Statistical Abstract,* 1979, p. 292.

10. *Regional Cycles and Employment Effects of Public Works Investments, and Public Works as Countercyclical Assistance.*

3

FINANCING PUBLIC WORKS IN THE '80s: THE COMPETITION FOR CAPITAL

In the 1980s, the competition for financial capital will be intense. The private sector will require substantial investment in order to regain its competitive edge in both domestic and international markets. The re-tooling and modernization of many of our basic industries is imperative. General Motors alone is now engaged in a five-year re-tooling effort that will cost over $40 billion. The capital requirements of high technology firms that will create a large portion of the jobs of the future will be still greater. But at the same time, our public infrastructure must be renovated and upgraded. Otherwise many of our efforts in economic renewal will be thwarted and community services will deteriorate even further.

At present it is difficult to even estimate the range of potential investments that will be required for public facilities. This reflects:(a) the absence of national capital budgeting; (b) the absence of common standards for public works facilities and the services they provide; (c) inadequate information on the inventory and condition of existing facilities and the costs of repair; and (d) the lack of a political consensus on what types of projects should receive priorities.

Even though the magnitude of the problem cannot be specified, it is obvious the public works investment requirements for the 1980s will far exceed the investment levels of the 1970s. Clearly not all needed projects can be funded. Too many other compelling public and private uses of capital exist. A number of difficult strategic choices must be made. The first is to determine how much of the Gross National Product (GNP) is to be allocated to consumption and how much encouraged into savings for new capital investment. The second is to determine how much of that capital investment will be used by the public sector and how much by the private sector. The third set of choices involves the allocation of what will inevitably be limited public works funds among specific places and classes of projects.

INVESTMENT VERSUS CONSUMPTION

For at least two decades, in both the public and private sectors, we have favored consumption over investment. Relative levels of the GNP devoted to real private sector investment in production have declined. So too have real levels of investment in public works. While the nation has been able to live off its past accomplishments for a brief period of time by deferring capital investment to subsidize current consumption, we have come to the point when maintaining even the status quo will require substantial increases in both the real levels of investment, public and private, and the share of GNP devoted to it.

Since the end of the Second World War, private sector fixed capital investment has been approximately 10 percent of the annual GNP.[1] But this figure masks a decline in real productive investment as the private sector has been forced by regulation to divert some of its capital into non-productive activities. For example, environmental investments made by private firms in the United States in 1979 exceeded $23 billion—10 percent of the total capital investment made that year by the private sector. Occupational safety and other regulations similarly diverted capital.

The diversion of this capital away from production-related activities would be of secondary consequence *if* there had been corresponding increases in the relative levels of the GNP devoted to capital investment. Unfortunately, there have not been. The share of GNP devoted to private sector fixed capital investment has not appreciably changed in recent years. As discussed in Chapter 2, the rate and levels of capital investment in public facilities has continuously dropped since the mid-1960s. Investment in public facilities accounted for 44 percent less of the GNP in 1977 than in 1965.

Increasing the shares of the GNP used for investment will strike hard at both public and private consumption. Many individuals will experience deferred growth in wages, dividends and other income and thus postponed personal consumption, while those resources flow into new facilities. Progress in environmental protection might also have to be slowed in order to increase the allocation of capital to productive investment. As distasteful as such sacrifices might be, they are certain to be much less painful than the long-term consequences that will result from the continued deterioration of the economy and the public facilities that undergird it.

CAPITAL ALLOCATIONS BETWEEN THE PRIVATE AND PUBLIC SECTORS

The allocation of investment capital between public and private uses raises a nettlesome challenge for the decade. Traditionally, government has been able to determine its share of capital through the preemptive use of its taxing and borrowing powers. Over the past five decades, government has also increased its role in promoting and enforcing a hierarchy of uses of capital *within* the private sector. Mandated safety and environmental investments are only a few of the many examples of government-encouraged or directed uses of private capital.

Rationalizing capital allocations among and between the private and public sectors will be difficult because: (1) public and private capital investments are intertwined; and (2) the present government interventions that influence capital allocations are random. In the 1980s, the federal government must reduce many of its influences over private investment decisions, let the "market" better work its will, and simultaneously define and adopt more coherent policies and management practices to guide those interventions affecting capital allocations that it must, of necessity, continue.

In a decade of intense competition for capital, governments at all levels will have to carefully assess the consequences of their interventions for economic productivity in general. They will also find it essential to carefully plan and budget the claims they must make in the capital market to finance the renovation and construction of public infrastructure essential to bolster that private productivity and provide essential community services.

Several actions will be necessary to meet these objectives:

■ Better uses of existing financing mechanisms and new approaches to the long-term financing of capital improvements will have to be explored.

■ To help establish true priorities for public works improvements, financing and use of facilities may have to be more clearly related to each other. Too often under the pluralism of our federal system, those who benefit from an improvement and those who pay are not the same. In some cases, that is defensible public policy. But often it is not.

■ Inefficiencies and fraud that waste a substantial share of each public works dollar must be substantially reduced or eliminated.

■ Rigorously drawn long-term capital budgets that can accommodate shorter-term counter-cyclical policies are essential if public facilities investments are to be disciplined so that they do not subvert private investment requirements in capital markets.

■ A clear definition of who is responsible for what will be essential to ensure full accountability and effectiveness. (What public facilities might be provided more effectively and efficiently through private firms? What are the public works responsibilities of the federal government that are distinct from those of state and local governments?)

CAPITAL ALLOCATION AMONG PLACES

The final and perhaps most sensitive— even volatile—sets of allocation choices concern the division of public works funds among places. In allocating public works funds among places two issues appear relevant. First, public works investments in themselves can do little to reverse structural economic change or induce individuals back to places they have left. Too many other forces are involved.

For example, even with decades of investment in rural areas, little was accomplished by attempts to alter the flow of persons and economic activity back into those areas. When such change finally did occur, it was largely the consequence of other more powerful demographic and economic forces such as people desiring retirement homes in warm climates and structural shifts in economic production due to alterations in factors of production such as costs of labor. These structural forces must be carefully identified and analyzed to determine their implications on public works policies. For example, rebuilding or even rehabilitating much of the infrastructure in many cities will not in itself offset such broader structural forces as the availability of energy, the costs of labor, or the transportation differentials created by shifting markets. In such circumstances strategies are required to help accommodate to smaller populations and different forms of economic growth. Such strategies should guide market forces by smoothing out their rough edges, rather than by attempting to reverse them. Public works investments should support new realities. This will not only ease the pains of transition and speed it along, it will also reduce the backlog of public works investments.

Setting priorities in the use of public works funds will be a neccesity in an era of increasingly scarce public resources. For example, should the nation complete the remaining 1,500 miles of the Interstate Highway System at approximately $75 billion of cost or use part of those funds to do all or some of the $33 billion of bridge repairs now needed, accelerate industrial water and waste water treatment facility construction, or some combination of these and other alternatives? Or should new construction with federal funds be de-emphasized to provide more balance with needs for rehabilitation, maintenance, and operations? While some parts of the nation, such as the South and West, require new facilities, other regions need funds for rehabilitation and maintenance.

FINANCING OUR PUBLIC WORKS NEEDS
Many states and localities have fallen back on the "soft" option—deferring maintenance in order to meet current operating costs and to balance their budgets. Now we are compelled to deal with the inevitable result of delayed upkeep: replacement, reconstruction, or abandonment.

As cities and states became dependent on intergovernmental grants-in-aid for capital investment (federal grants provided ten percent of state-local capital expenditures in 1957, but now exceed 40 percent), they grew highly susceptible to the biases reflected in federal programs.[2] The most pronounced of these biases has been towards new construction. Many federal programs do not permit the use of funds for main-

33

tenance. Substantial under-maintenance has resulted in many fiscally stressed cities. Pagano and Moore found that those public works activities financed by user charges are far less susceptible to inadequate maintenance than those financed from general funds, particularly in fiscally distressed cities.[3] Boston and New Orleans, with dedicated revenue sources, were better able to maintain water services and facilities than other cities using general revenues.

The choice of mixes in the use of limited funds among types of public works projects and among the various public works functions is made difficult in the absence of: (1) a framework for decisions; (2) basic information on the existence of facilities, the quality of services they provide, and construction/service standards; and (3) cost estimates. Such limitations seriously cripple efforts to assess the consequences of these decisions on both the private sector and other government functions.

The potential sources of public works financing such as privatization, user charges, debt financing, and tax-based federal, state, and local financing require a careful re-examination. For example, substantial increases in certain forms of local taxes to finance public works may deter private sector investment. Conversely, an increase in federal public works expenditures may require reductions in other federal state and local expenditures unless better modes of financing are developed.

The federal government finances many of the public works for which it is directly responsible through direct appropriations, such as those for the Corps of Engineers. Others it finances out of capital markets such as those of the Tennessee Valley Authority. Many cities are being forced out of the bond market because of high interest rates, a "tightness" caused by the sale of pollution control bonds, and the expanded and often promiscuous use of industrial revenue bonds. Many smaller communities are also finding that small bond issues present such high transaction costs (law fees, underwriting expenses, printing, etc.) that they are effectively excluded from the market. A number of ways exist to facilitate access to private bond markets by smaller communities. One is the creation of consolidated bond sales (several communities going together in order to reduce transaction costs). A number of states, such as Florida, have supported such efforts and have established the necessary financing mechanisms to achieve this goal.

National, regional, or state "development banks" have been proposed from time to time to improve access to capital markets and lower transaction costs. The National Public Advisory Committee on Regional Development reviewed the diverse array of options for creating a National Development Bank and a potential Reconstruction Finance Corporation. After public hearings and analysis, that body of public officials, bankers, and public administrators concluded that such a mechanism is needed and if created should operate much like the Federal Land Bank. It should provide *access* to capital markets for communities and states (particularly smaller places), should *only* be used for capital construction or rehabilitation, and should charge interest rates which reflect *market* prices. The advantage of such a mechanism would be *guaranteed* access to monies for needed facilities, reduced transaction costs, a long-term pay back schedule, and the longer-term capitalization of some interest in order to provide "patient" capital in the early years of a project's life.[4]

Since about half of all federal funds for public works are disbursed to state and local governments for improvements, administrative requirements under these programs must be evaluated to determine their influences on the renovation of vital infrastructure. Requirements that investments be targeted on needy neighborhoods under the Community Development Block Grant Program have prevented the use of these funds for renovation of urban infrastructure on any scale significant to economic renewal.[5]

Increased Application   While user charges are an accustomed
of User Charges   method of financing many public services, there are many instances in which their expanded and creative use could result in more effective financing and more efficient management.

The General Accounting Office's (GAO) analysis of the need for additional federal aid for urban water distribution systems concluded that, where fee-for-service financing existed, as in Boston and New Orleans, management was better.[6] Actions were taken to improve conservation, reduce leakage, and control other non-revenue producing water uses, such as illegal hydrant openings and meter under-registration. Conversely, cities such as Washington, D.C., whose water programs are financed from general revenues, give little attention to leakage or even such issues as more consistent collection of existing water fees. For example, the GAO found that in 1972, 35 percent of Washington, D.C.'s water distribution mains needed replacement, cleaning, or lining. By 1980, over 50 percent of these mains required reconstruction.

In the southwestern United States, the sale of municipal water is often a principal source of community revenues—particularly in smaller communities.

The use of fee-for-service charges improves access to capital markets because of a dedicated, guaranteed flow of revenues. They also have the virtue of more directly relating prices to consumption and real costs. Many cities, such as New York City, do not meter sales of water. Metering would eliminate much waste and could obviate some of the demand for construction of expensive, supplemental supply systems. Where the cost of providing meters is prohibitive, other alternatives

35

can be devised. User charges can adversely affect low income citizens, but in those circumstances, special income adjustments for the poor can be created.

Privatizing Public Facilities

Still another alternative worthy of consideration is private operation of some facilities that in recent decades have been the responsibility of the public sector. Earlier in this century, the private construction and operation of water supply systems was common. More recently, we have seen private contractors as alternatives in the delivery of many services to public agencies. Competition in garbage collection, fire protection, street cleaning, and parcel delivery are examples. This model can apply to the construction and operation of many kinds of public facilities as well.

The Advisory Commission on Intergovernmental Relations (ACIR) and the International City Managers Association (ICMA) have both conducted surveys to measure cities' reliance on and preference for the use of private sector firms to provide select public services.[7] Of 2,650 cities surveyed by ACIR, over 36 percent of the respondents indicated a preference for contracting with a private firm for the provision of services rather than shifting or giving the responsibilities to government agencies. The ICMA survey of 379 cities determined that 225 respondents were already using private firms in their productivity programs—particularly in solid waste collection and disposal; street maintenance and construction; hospital construction and operation; and public transit.

The use of private firms is influenced by a number of historical, political, and economic considerations. Many cities are using private firms for waste collection and disposal because private firms can secure necessary capital funds irrespective of local expenditure limits. In the past many hospitals were established by or purchased by communities because of the inability of the private sector to raise necessary capital. Today, with revenue generating abilities of government increasingly constrained, such facilities are starting to revert back to private ownership and operation.

Private firms provide a means to escape the excessive rigidities of overly-bureaucratized public agencies and public labor-management problems. Private firms can sometimes be more efficient and operate at less cost than public agencies because of their ability to swiftly introduce new technology; their greater flexibility in the use of worker incentives; their ability to eliminate or reduce an unneeded service by simply not continuing a contract; and their often superior understanding of economies of scale and specialization. The ability of private firms to provide better, less costly services will vary between specific functions and areas.

The potential for privatizing public services must be gauged realistically. It is wise to remember that many facilities and services once privately and now publicly provided were converted because of abuse and corruption in the private sector and many private sector operations are inching slowly toward the public sector today. The conversion of many of the bankrupt railroads into quasi-public entities such as CONRAIL and AMTRAK are but two of the more glaring reminders. Federal loan guarantees to major corporations in economic trouble provide more evidence of this drift in the other direction.

Privatization is not an option in all circumstances. There will always be situations in which the private sector is unable to provide profitably many basic services such as water, electricity, or waste disposal. The arguments most often advanced against the use of privatization include:

■ Poorer service and greater consumer expense because of the need for profits.
■ Problems of controlling, monitoring and evaluating the performance of contractors.
■ Private sector graft—collusion among bidders and bribery of public officials.
■ Problems of preparing enforceable contracts.
■ The often fierce opposition from government workers and unions.

The U.S. Chamber of Commerce suggests five basic steps for exploring the potential of privatization:
■ Identify to what extent federal, state and local laws restrict or promote the use of private firms for the provision of select services.
■ Determine if there are a sufficient number of firms qualified to provide the service under reasonable terms.
■ Ascertain whether bidding and procurement procedures are so formidable that private firms will be deterred.
■ Determine whether public authorities are given preference over private firms.
■ Determine if adequate and reasonable performance measures have been identified. If performance or incentive contracts are to be used, such standards are absolutely necessary. However, without such standards, any firm providing such services would either be at risk or the public sector would risk not getting their money's worth.[8]

There is limited information on the effectiveness of privatization and the specific circumstances in which it is most appropriate. There is also limited agreement on which types of facilities and services should be provided by the private sector. Yet privatization offers a potentially important means for government to move toward a system in which public facilities and services receive priorities reflected in the realities of what the market will support. It also has the virtue of relating more directly those who pay with those who benefit.

Interim Privatization

There are other alternatives. One is to grant licenses and rights of eminent domain to an authority or private company to permit them to finance and construct a facility, operate it with user charges until the investment is returned and a profit is secured, and then turn ownership over to the public. The major highway between Dallas and Fort Worth, Texas was financed, built, and operated in this manner.

A more extensive privatization scheme has been suggested by *The Economist* for use in Great Britain.[9] It is applicable in the United States as well. The private sector would construct, rehabilitate, maintain, and operate a city's sewers or streets or municipal buildings with debt which is privately raised and held. The city would repay the cost of the debt over a fixed period of time, such as 10 or 20 years, at the end of which the government would own the facility.

This arrangement could be attractive to the private sector—and not only for its likely tax advantages by collateralizing select facilities and income flows. By earmarking user fees and being willing to guarantee where necessary limited annual supplemental payments, the private firms would be assured of securing excellent financial ratings and lowered borrowing costs. For cities with poor bond ratings, these savings could be substantial.

Such an approach would be attractive to communities for several reasons. First, necessary capital expenditures could be made more quickly than otherwise possible, particularly in hard-pressed places. Second, assigning a private firm the responsibilities to collect user charges and maintain the facility would likely result in both a higher collection rate and better maintained facilities. Third, such financing could reduce the financing burdens placed on city budgets.

But it is unlikely that the public sector will be willing to accept departures in present policies unless it can be assured of more effective uses of public works dollars than the present policies and practices have yielded.

FOOTNOTES TO CHAPTER 3

1. *Being Number One: Rebuilding the U.S. Economy.*

2. *A Study of Public Works Investment in the United States,* p. 15.

3. Pagano, Michael, A., and Moore Richard J., "Emerging Issues in Financing Basic Infrastructure," an unpublished paper, 1980.

4. United States Department of Commerce, *Recommendations of the National Public Advisory Committee on Regional Development,* Washington, D.C., 1977.

5. Henry, Patrick J., "Removing Internal Restrictions in the CDBG Program to Permit More Creative Uses by Local Governments," an unpublished paper, the Academy for Contemporary Problems, Washington, D.C., November, 1980.

6. *Additional Federal Aid for Urban Water Distribution Systems Should Wait Until Needs are Clearly Established.* p. i–v.

7. The Chamber of Commerce of the United States, *Improving Local Government Fiscal Management,* Washington, D.C., pp. 32–35.

8. *Improving Local Government Fiscal Management.*

9. The Economist, "How to Privatise Public Investment," London, United Kingdom, December 5, 1980, p. 20.

4

GETTING MORE FOR THE PUBLIC WORKS DOLLAR: REDUCING THE COST OF DELAY

The nation can get much more from the public works dollars it is spending. To do so, we must attack:

■ The losses resulting from delay (about one-fifth of the $80 billion in annual public works appropriations);

■ The losses resulting from the misuse of funds; and

■ The losses resulting from wasteful management and bad planning.

THE COSTS OF DELAY

In the 1960s, an electric power plant could be constructed in less than five years. Today, more than 12 years are required. The Tennessee Valley Authority (TVA) is currently experiencing an average eight-year delay in seven major power plants—a delay which has almost trebled construction costs by raising costs an additional $11 billion.[1] This is a good example of what happens when we neglect the consequences of mismanaging time. Time is, indeed, money.

The time consumed in building major projects is increasingly determined by government regulations and requirements. Yet, public administrators have tended to be ignorant of or insensitive to the costs and consequences of delays in their administrative, financial, regulatory and legal decisions. Unnecessary delays are decreasing real capital investment as funds are diverted to the nonproductive task of financing increased interest charges generated when projects take longer to put into operation. Additional funds are required to keep pace with inflation-devalued public works purchasing power as delays put off construction. Financing delay has become a major levy on available monies for public works. About 20 percent ($16 billion) of the nation's annual public works appropriations are now used for such financing—a major and unnecessary waste of shrinking public capital.[2]

Yet, in the past, government and business have often successfully met tight schedules. An American was placed on the Moon in less than a decade. The new Smithsonian Air and Space Museum was constructed on time and under budget. But to ensure that such performance becomes the norm rather than the exception, major reforms are needed.

There are no reliable statistics on the time allocated to the many

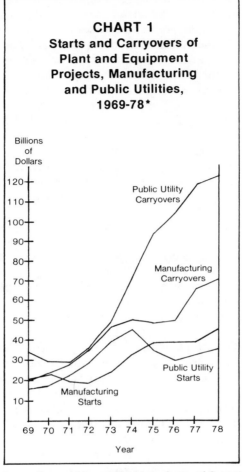

CHART 1
Starts and Carryovers of Plant and Equipment Projects, Manufacturing and Public Utilities, 1969-78*

Billions of Dollars

Public Utility Carryovers

Manufacturing Carryovers

Public Utility Starts

Manufacturing Starts

Year

Source: Bureau of Economic Analysis, **Survey of Current Business**, June, 1969–78.

*Starts represent new construction. Carryovers represent expenditures to be incurred for plant and equipment at the end of the first quarter of each year.

phases of public works projects, i.e., research, design financing, and approval. However, there is reliable information on the construction phase in both the public and private sectors. Since the mid-1960s, the Bureau of Economic Analysis of the Department of Commerce has annually reported the aggregate value of public and private construction starts, as well as the cumulative value of uncompleted construction carried over into each new year (Chart 1).

In the period 1969-1978, the Bureau reported substantial increases in the value of annual construction carry-overs, which reflect (1) increases in the cost of starts; (2) increases in the costs of projects; and (3) the additional time required to complete projects.

The most spectacular increase of carry-overs compared to the value of starts has been in public utility construction. In 1969, there were about $19 billion in carry-overs from 1968 and about $15 billion in new public utility starts. This represented a ratio of carry-overs to starts of 1.2 to 1. By 1978, there were approximately $122 billion in carry-overs from 1977, and $35 billion in new starts. Thus, within a decade, the carry-over-to-starts ratio in this industry has almost tripled, rising to 3.5 to 1. In large measure these delays were due to the dramatic expansion of time required to complete new electric generating plants—five years in the late 1960s as compared with 12 years a decade later.

Another measure of delay can be obtained by analyzing the time lags in the disbursements of funds for public construction programs. Presently, many agencies require six or more years to disburse a single fiscal year's appropriations—even after the funds have been committed to specific projects (Table 11). For example, although the Economic Development Administration has one of the federal government's better construction management programs, projects now require one year between approval and construction bids. By contrast the GAO found that of the 77 projects for which the Corps of Engineers completed survey investigation or design phases during fiscal years 1975, 1976, and 1977, an average of *26 years* was required after initial authorization before construction began. Over 12 years were used for planning and 14 years for reviews and appropriations.[3] HUD's Community Development Block Grant Program has a construction backlog equal to three years of that program's annual budget for construction.[4] The Environmental Protection Agency has a backlog of construction projects exceeding $8 billion—a backlog equal to two full years of appropriations.[5] Many public works projects funded at least a decade ago are still unfinished.

Similar delays are found in virtually all federal, state, and local public works construction programs. In aggregate, the value of projects in the public works pipeline now exceeds over $100 billion (Table 12).

CAUSES OF DELAY

In a complex world, some delay is justified to allow the consequences of an action to be adequately considered. But managerial indifference is too often the cause. This indifference is often equated with "prudence," or with being a "part of the system." Consequently, little is done to bring delay under control. Instead, poor planning, unbounded time consumed in decisionmaking, changing regulations, increased

Table 11

Disbursement Rates for the Community Development Block Grant Program, Local Public Works, and the Economic Development Administration's Title I Public Works Programs

Year	CDBG [a]	LPW [b]	EDA - Title I [c]
	Rate at Which One Year of Funding is Disbursed		
1	2.6	9.75	4.2
2	30.2	50.95	29.9
3	48.3	29.00	39.9
4	15.4	5.97	4.4
5	5.5	3.33	7.7
6	0	1.0	5.7

a. The Department of Housing and Urban Development's Community Development Block Grant Program. These data include both construction and non-construction activities. At present, this program has a backlog of approximately $6 billion—about one-third of the total funds appropriated since FY 1974. Of this backlog approximately 55 percent are earmarked for construction. Since this program invests only 25-30 percent of its annual appropriations in capital items, the backlog represents almost three years of capital funding.

b. LPW disbursement rates are calculated from the budgetary data presented in the *Budget of the United States* for the years 1977-81. Since the LPW program was initiated in the middle of two different fiscal years, these data are an aggregate of the speed with which funds were expended.

c. EDA Public Works drawndown rates are calculated on the basis of EDA disbursements as of January 15, 1980. Since these calculations are based upon the first quarter of FY 1980, these estimates slightly overstate the disbursement rates of the program. The EDA totals do not add to 100 since there are funds as yet undisbursed for fiscal years prior to FY 1974.

litigation, and chaotic administration are the real culprits in expanding the time required to plan and construct necessary public works projects.

Pre-Construction Delays

The primary source of construction delays is found in the pre-construction stage of projects. Essentially the sources of these construction delays are:

■ *Lack of Specific Time Limits*—Many regulatory functions are conducted with virtually no time limits. For example, licensing or zoning applications may pend for years before decisions are rendered. Government actually encourages delay, since there are high penalties for government officials if mistakes are made in accelerating projects.

■ *Institutional Fragmentation*—Often, more than one government agency is involved in a specific project or activity. For example, most

Table 12
The Value of the Public Works Pipeline
(Billions of Dollars)

Fiscal Year	Value of Public Works	Present Value of Backlog
1980	$ 45.0	$ 43.7
1979	45.0	30.2
1978	45.0	10.4
1977	43.4	5.6
1976-70	249.1	14.9
TOTAL	$487.5	$101.8

SOURCE: These are estimated values. The base value of the public works pipeline is the actual amount of capital construction expenditures as reported by the U.S. Bureau of the Census in the *Statistical Abstract of the United States, 1979* for all governments (federal, state, and local)—Table 478. This value does not include land costs or most equipment included in these projects. The value of public works construction for 1978 is unpublished data supplied by the Census. Values for 1979 and 1980 are estimates.

The present value of the national public works backlog is calculated on the basis of the following disbursement rates: Year 1—3 percent; Year 2—30 percent; Year 3—44 percent; Year 4—10 percent; Year 5—7 percent; and Years 6-10—a residual rate of 6 percent. These disbursements rates are the average of those found in public works programs of the Department of Commerce's Economic Development Administration and the Department of Housing and Urban Development's Community Development Block Grant Program.

These estimates are based on the value of the backlog as of 1 October 1980.

public works projects require at least 16 federal certifications—many from a variety of agencies and many of which have different procedures and criteria for decisionmaking.

Also decisions are often made at different managerial levels and in different geographic locations. The conflicts created by this fragmentation are almost always left to the state and local governments to resolve.

■ *Documentation Delay*—All levels of government require documentation for public works projects. Often state and local requirements are more time consuming than their federal counterparts.

■ *Judicial Delays*—A wide array of legislation gives citizens and public interest groups easy access to court action. Often suits are filed by opponents of projects to delay construction and to shift costs so as to assure that a project never leaves the drawing board.

Although responsibility for pre-construction delays is shared by all levels of governments, an increasing body of evidence suggests that much of it is at the local level. An analysis of delays in the construction grants program of the Environmental Protection Agency has identified four fundamental sources of pre-construction delays: (1) real property acquisitions (including easements); (2) lack of local funding; (3) difficulty in negotiating service agreements; and (4) slow historical resource investigations.[6]

The Department of Housing and Urban Development's Community Development Block Grant (CDBG) has experienced similar delays with local governments, and has concluded that the primary causes for delays were (1) inadequate local project planning; and (2) local bureaucratic red tape (Table 13).

The delays caused by inadequate planning reflect the fact that at the local level many federal grants for specific local public works projects are made on the basis of "concepts" rather than actual projects. More specifically, funds are provided for a project idea; the community then produces a detailed plan, secures architectural and engineering designs, gets clearances and approvals, secures local funds, buys land, lets bids, and awards contracts. During this preparatory period, the project funds remain warehoused, and lose purchasing power as inflation erodes their value.

Implementation of the CDBG program at the local level has been hindered by numerous interagency procedures, local approval requirements, and local political conflicts. HUD also found most local governments to be well-versed in the requirements of the federal government, such as Bacon-Davis standards and environmental protection rules, but often ignorant of their own local and state laws and regulations.

Delays in the Construction Process Actual delays in constructing a project are a minor source of the overall delay. There are exceptions, of course, such as the construction of the new Hart Senate Office Building, which will require seven to ten years to complete. However, the majority of the public works projects require only 6 to 21 months to complete once construction begins. (Table 14).

THE CONSEQUENCES OF DELAYED PUBLIC WORKS CONSTRUCTION

Unnecessary delays have many direct and and indirect effects on the national economy, including diminished purchasing power and productivity growth; postponed benefits; uncertainty and a loss of confidence in the public sector.

45

Table 13

Principal Delay Factors in the Community Development Block Grant Program

Factors Associated With Project Start Up	Factors Associated With Project Approval	Factors Associated With Project Operation
Local approval requirements (e.g., commission and legislative bodies)	Local political debate over project (e.g., involving major/council/commissioners)	Civil rights compliance
		Davis-Bacon requirements
Condemnation process preceding acquisition	Citizen complaints	State requirements
		Staff capabilities
Environmental review process	Lawsuits	
Citizen participation process	Negotiations with HUD	Project costs
Administrative factors (inter-agency cooperation, contracting procedures, etc.)		Local bookkeeping methods for transfer of funds
Arrival of other federal funds to match		Urban county procedures for reimbursing cooperating jurisdictions
Need to secure private financial commitments		
Planning, design, and implementation after HUD approval		
Urban renewal local approval requirements		
Weather		

Source: Unpublished data, U.S. Department of Housing and Urban Development, Washington, D.C., 1980.

Diminished
Purchasing Power
Delay diminishes purchasing power during a period of inflation. For at least the the past decade the rate of inflation in the construction industry has been higher than general price increases. Thus delayed projects become more costly to build—diverting funds from other potential uses. At present the backlog of public works in the United States that have been funded, but are not yet completed or under construction, represent a $100 billion pool of funds that is diminishing in value every day. In such a circumstance delay is very expensive in terms of lost purchasing power.

Postponed Benefits
When delay postpones the benefits of projects, economic and social side effects can be serious. For example, as the TVA has had to postpone its construction of new power plants, it has both substantially increased capital costs and deferred the operation of a major source of nonpetroleum electric generation.

San Bernadino's experience in delaying construction of a series of community and service centers for the elderly is another example of postponed benefits *and* the loss of purchasing power. In 1975, that county government decided to build the centers for the elderly, but elected to accumulate construction funds for them at the rate of one-third of total project costs per year. By the time the funds were accumulated, the county found the monies it had set aside were inadequate to finance the program—inflation had done its magic. Thus, the county was obliged to decide whether to reduce the size of the centers, to cancel some of them, or to divert funds from other projects to complete the project.

Uncertainty and
Loss of Confidence
Major public works projects are increasingly affected by litigation, by changing social and political conditions, by changing technology, by changing public regulatory actions, and by inflation. As the time required to complete a project is extended, the project is exposed to increasing uncertainties and risks.

The construction of any major waterway, flood control project, mass transit system, reservoir, or highway provides examples of projects initiated and constructed under conditions of growing uncertainty. As time needed for pre-construction activities continues to expand, construction cost containment is virtually impossible. Construction firms cannot negotiate long-term, fixed-fee contracts because of inflation. Also regulatory requirements change and there is little assurance that today's requirements will be the same tomorrow.

Moreover, major projects require political, social and economic accord which is difficult to maintain when conditions of uncertainty exist.

47

Table 14
Duration of Construction, by Type of Public Works Project

	Duration segments (months)	Total Duration in Months	Total On-site Man-hours[a]	Range of Construction Time
Building Construction				
Private one-family housing		4.8	37.5	NA
Public housing	10.4, 21.6, 27.3, 23.2, 15.1	14.8	52.9	NA
Schools	15.6, 26.9, 32.6, 22.2	12.0	39.3	NA
Hospitals	6.5, 12.4, 16.5, 19.3, 17.6, 14.9, 9.8, 3.0	21.0	43.4	10-47
Nursing		13.4	42.0	NA
College housing	11.1, 22.4, 31.3, 25.4, 9.6	13.4	43.7	4-22
Federal office buildings	6.8, 15.3, 20.5, 23.0, 21.8, 12.0, .6	16.8	41.9	9-31
Heavy Construction				
Sewer lines	27.0, 41.1, 26.4, 5.5	9.5	45.0	NA
Sewer plants	45.7, 47.3	6.5	43.4	NA
Land operations[b]	27.5, 33.5, 26.0, 13.0	11.1	52.2	2-30
Dredging[c]	39.5, 44.0, 16.5	6.7	82.3	2-16

Bar chart horizontal scale (months): 3, 6, 9, 12, 15, 18, 21

48

Sources: *Labor and Material Requirements for Construction of Private Single-Family Houses, 1972,* BLS Bulletin 1755, p. 5; *Labor and Material Requirements for Public Housing Construction 1968, 1974,* BLS Bulletin 1821, pp. 6-7;*Labor and Material Requirements for School Construction, June 1968,* BLS Bulletin 1586, pp. 7, 17; *Labor and Material Requirements for Hospital and Nursing Home Construction, 1971,* BLS Bulletin 1691, pp. 14-15; *Labor and Material Requirements for College Housing Construction, May 1965,* BLS Bulletin 1441, pp. 24-25; *Labor Requirements for Federal Office Building Construction, 1962,* BLS Bulletin 1331, pp. 26-27; *Labor and Material Requirements for Sewer Works Construction, 1966,* Bulletin 1490, p. 18; *Labor and Material Requirements for Civil Works Construction by the Corps of Engineers, 1964,* BLS Bulletin 1390, pp. 19-20.

NOTES: Figures in italics indicate percentage of total on-site man-hours spent in quarter. NA means not available.

a. For each $1000 of contract costs, measured in 1974 dollars.

b. Land operations, as defined by the Bureau of Labor Statistics, include 28 civil works projects: large earth-filled dams (3 projects), small earth-filled dams (1 project), small earth-filled dams (3 projects), local flood protection (3 projects), pile dikes (5 projects), levees (7 projects), revetments (5 projects), and four miscellaneous projects—channel improvement, jetties, outlet channel, and sea wall extension.

c. Dredging includes 15 projects, of two different types: hydraulic, in which a dredge equipped with a cutterhead pumps soft material through a pipeline to a disposal area, usually on-shore; and the second type, in which soft or broken hard material is loaded into scows and taken to a disposal area, usually in deep water. The sample projects are the same as those used in the Haveman and Krutilla study.

Source: Vernez, Georges; Vaughn, Roger; Burright, Burke; and Coleman Sinclair, *Regional Cycles and Employment Effects of Public Works Investments,* The Rand Corporation, Santa Monica, California, January 1977.

49

The private sector is affected by uncertainty as well. Firms are reluctant to invest in ventures dependent on public infrastructure that is either nonexistent or in poor repair. Ultimately, uncertainty causes a loss of public confidence in government and in government leaders.

REFORMS   Unnecessary delays can be eliminated. Several basic reforms are necessary to control time management—some of them can be accomplished quickly; others will take time. All are important.

Short-Term Actions   The first and most needed short-term action is to reduce the $100 billion backlog in the public works pipeline. Since the majority of the funds in this backlog represents appropriated, but unused federal funds, the principal responsibility for identifying and initiating reforms resides with the Office of Management and Budget and the respective federal agencies. State and local agencies should be involved when appropriate. The following actions might be taken:

1. Identify the backlog of public works obligations by fiscal year, by specific project, and by specific funding agency.

2. Divide these obligated, but undisbursed, funds into five categories:

A. Projects which are permanently stalled.

B. Projects which are salvageable, but are stalled due to a variety of factors (lack of local matching funds; inability to meet regulatory requirements; rising construction costs; etc.).

C. Projects under construction but which could be accelerated in order to reduce or eliminate further delay.

D. Projects that are on schedule but which require no action.

E. Projects on schedule but which could be accelerated.

Those projects already funded which appear to be terminally stalled should be closely assessed by the individual funding agencies. If there is no, or only a remote, possibility that these individual projects will enter the construction stage within a specific time, such as nine months, the funds allocated to these projects should be de-obligated and re-programmed so that other projects can make use of these funds.

In order that communities with stalled projects are not unduly penalized, the funding agency could create procedures for re-funding the project within a specified period of time, such as two years. During that period, the community would have the right to re-assess the project. If it is determined to be still feasible and all requirements for construction are met, the de-obligated project would be given priority status for re-funding consideration.

Funds freed under such a de-obligation process could then be channeled to other projects ready for construction, could be used to fund new projects, or could be used to supplement existing programs which have been halted by inflation.

The backlogs under block grant programs, such as the CDBG of HUD and facilities grants from EPA, could be reduced through the use of a forward-funding concept. Using such an approach, communities able to use construction funds expeditiously could request and receive advance funding based on their future entitlements. Advance funds would come from the agency's existing backlog.

The expenditure of funded block grant programs, such as HUD's CDBG program and the construction programs of EPA, would produce substantial benefits including:

■ Increased purchasing power.

■ Improved services to the public.

■ Counter-cyclical employment in construction and construction-related industries.

A sound management action that can be taken is to identify systematically impediments to the construction of funded projects. These impediments should be analyzed to determine:

■ Their nature and source.

■ Organizations responsible for the delays.

■ Actions necessary to reduce or eliminate delays.

■ A timetable for project completion.

■ Actions necessary to change legislation, policies and operating procedures to eliminate future delays.

Such analysis could be rapidly completed given the expertise that does exist in the public works agencies.

Long-Term Actions   A number of long-term policy and administrative reforms to improve time management are both possible and appropriate. This can (1) reduce delay, and (2) minimize the cost of those delays which do occur.

Improved time management will involve many actions, some of which may seem unimportant but which in aggregate will reduce delay. For example, HUD has prepared a guide for local officials on streamlining land use regulations.[7] This guide identifies many small but important steps local officials can take to simplify land development reviews at the pre-application stage, at the staff review stage, and at the public official review stage. Many of these actions are simple, commonsense approaches—such as arranging an early pre-application conference between the applicant and staff persons from the reviewing departments of local government. The identification and resolution of dozens of small impediments can substantially reduce delay.

The following basic measures, coupled with dozens, even hundreds, of other ingenious implementing actions, can make substantial contributions to reducing government-induced delay.

■ *Creation of Public Works Time Management Standards and Monitoring Procedures.* Time management standards and procedures are needed throughout government. Reliable and consistent indicators for decisionmaking and government action can be established relatively inexpensively. When such information is available to administrators, to the Congress, and to the public, it will be possible to identify policy and administrative changes which can enhance program effectiveness and efficiency. A number of basic indicators are required for the creation of effective standards:

a. Chronological data are needed on time requirements for construction of various types of public works projects. These data will help in finding the causes for delay.

b. Time limitations for all applications for government funds should be established.

c. Deadlines should be established and monitored for the time consumed between project funding and actual expenditure.

d. Unexpended balances of funds in each program for present and past fiscal years must also be monitored. Using this information, accurate norms for expenditure rates could be created. Deviations would indicate the need for policy or administrative changes. These data are already available in each public works agency, but a standard format and reporting system are lacking.

■ *Create Personal and Institutional Incentive.* Among other considerations, public managers and employees must be rewarded or penalized according to how well they manage time.

Beneficiaries of federal and state grant-in-aid programs also need incentives for expeditious use of grants and other funds. Several such incentives are possible, and could include "use it or lose it" provisions linked to specific time frames and qualitative considerations. The impediment to such "either/or" incentives is legislation which does not permit reallocation of funds. For example, if EDA makes a public works grant commitment and the fiscal year ends before the funds are expended, those funds cannot be reallocated. If reprogramming were permitted, communities with inordinately slow expenditure rates could lose their grants and the unused monies transferred to areas where funds could be put to immediate use. The very existence of reprogramming possibilities could serve as an incentive to action. The effectiveness of this approach has been demonstrated in the Appalachian Regional Development Program.

Another possible means for creating incentives and simultaneously ensuring the efficient expenditures of funds is the use of previously described "forward-funding." Forward-funding would permit well managed communities to complete projects more rapidly, thus avoiding cost overruns caused by inflation. Slow draw-down communities would not be penalized more than they already are by their delays since they would retain the right to their entitlements. Their penalty would be the receipt of inflation-ravaged funds. At present levels of inflation, EPA would secure at least $1 billion of increased purchasing power annually from its $8 billion backlog by such an improved money management plan. This approach can be adapted by virtually every federal grant agency.

Agencies should also limit the amount of their funds that can be used for overruns. In most federal public works programs, over ten percent of all new public works funds are used to finance overruns on prior commitments. If the financing of overruns is shifted to state government and local communities, incentives for the expeditious use of funds are created. However, where delay is caused by the federal government, it should bear overrun costs.

■ *Improved Planning of Government Actions.* Government activities are often poorly planned. Short time horizons are the norm rather than the exception. Often little attention is given to indirect consequences of policies or actions. A major reform in HUD programs has been to require communities receiving CDBG funds to prepare a threeyear plan for projected use of these monies. This improved planning permits better citizen participation, better project consideration, and the more expeditious use of funds when they do become available. This form of planning is one of several reasons why HUD in the past two years has been able to accelerate the use of its funds.

The creation of two-step funding is another major innovation that would expedite the use of actual project funds. Small amounts of funds—as little as two percent of project costs—can be set aside very early for engineering, preliminary regulatory requirements and securing local matching funds. Major project funds would not be extended until these requisites had been met. Thus, when major funds are made available, they can be immediately used rather than being stored for one to three years. This pre-planning can significantly reduce delay and assist government to keep its money at work in projects—thus getting more for each dollar committed.

■ *Creation of Mediation Processes.* The federal government has long sponsored the Federal Mediation Service in the Department of Labor. This service uses both staff and consultants to assist in neutral mediation between management and labor. Using a variety of techniques they have assisted in resolving conflicts in hundreds of situations which otherwise would have been long delayed.

The mediation service is needed for public works and other projects which are stalled because of conflict. Examples of the range of disputes which can be settled through mediation are found in the experiences of the Institute for Environmental Mediation located in Seattle,

Washington. For example, a 1977 mediation process broke a six-year port development stalemate between development and environment advocates and the Port of Everett, Washington and a comprehensive development plan was created which was acceptable to all parties.

■ *Time-Bound Regulatory, Certification, Compliance and Permit Procedures.* Regulatory, certification, compliance, and permit procedures *must* have time limits. These limits must be reasonable, publicized, and firmly applied. When the limits are exceeded, the direct and indirect costs of delay should be calculated and individuals and organizations held responsible.

The federal government should require that *all* bureaucratic procedures be accomplished within specific time frames. This requirement, if further reinforced by legislation, would eliminate the burden of open-ended governmental decisionmaking on the construction industry in particular and on the business community in general.

■ *Simplify Government Regulatory, Certification, Compliance and Permit Procedures.* Regulatory, certification, compliance, and permit procedures need simplification. New York State has simplified the permit process for the private sector through the creation of an Office of Business Permits. This Office has a central inventory which identifies individual regulatory bodies in New York State, the types of activities for which permits are required, criteria for approval, costs involved, and the time required to secure permits. It also provides assistance to firms in meeting these requirements. Simultaneously it works with all state agencies, reviewing their permit processes in order to further simplify procedures and eliminate outmoded and burdensome requirements. Actions to create a simplified public works construction permit could include:

a. Creation of Office of Business Permits in most states to assist contractors in quickly meeting their requisites.

b. Simplification of federal, state and local certification and compliance requirements. This is an area with much potential for reducing delay. Presently, individual government agencies often have differing compliance requirements for the same legislation. Communities and businesses bear the direct expense and the cost of delay involved in meeting these multiple compliance and assurance standards which should be standarized so one certification is accepted by many agencies. Several federal agencies have begun this process in their funding of rural water and sewer projects. This overall responsibility would best be performed by OMB. It should be made one of the top priority items on OMB's agenda.

■ *Simplify and Streamline Appellate Procedures.* The appeals process requires simplification and streamlining. Under present laws and practices, motions to appeal government regulatory decisions are generally decided by the courts. Generally, these actions begin at the lower court level in the federal or state judicial system and work their way upward. Present appeals processes are time consuming, since fixed time schedules are rarely used. The process is made even more difficult and time consuming since appeals can be initiated in one of the many courts (scattered in several locations) with judges having little or no technical background on the questions at issue. There are a number of working models that could be adopted to expedite the appellate review process without sacrificing any quality of decisions—perhaps even improving the quality and consistency of decisions. For example, a streamlined appellate review process could be established. In such an approach, all appeals from permit or regulatory decisions in connection with a single development activity, such as land use regulation, could be combined in a single appellate review process. This would permit not only more expeditious decisions, but also the use of specialized staff and thus better decisions. Streamlined appellate processes can be structured while assuring access to all interested parties and therefore significantly reducing unnecessary and costly delay.

FOOTNOTES TO CHAPTER 4

1. Choate, Pat, *As Time Goes By: The Costs and Consequences of Delay,* The Academy for Contemporary Problems, Washington, D.C., 1980.

2. This is a calculated value based on a backlog of construction of $100 billion, an average delay per project of one year, construction and related inflation at 12 percent per year and interest rates for interim construction at 12 percent.

3. General Accounting Office, *Ways to Resolve Critical Water Resources Issues Facing the Nation,* Washington, D.C., p. 7.

4. United States Department of Housing and Urban Development, *CDBG Program Status by Government Unit,* Working Report, Washington, D.C., January, 1980.

5. United States Environmental Protection Agency, *Construction Grant Projects Not Under Construction,* Washington, D.C., June, 1980.

6. United States Environmental Protection Agency, *An Internal Analysis of the Causes of Construction Delays in the Construction Grant Projects,* (unpublished), Washington, D.C., 1980.

7. United States Department of Housing and Urban Development, *Local Capital Improvements and Development Management,* Washington, D.C., June, 1980.

5

GETTING MORE FOR THE PUBLIC WORKS DOLLAR: REDUCING FRAUD AND ADMINISTRATIVE WASTE

The precise magnitude of the funds lost through fraudulent practices or poor construction is impossible to estimate. The number of indictments and convictions for public works related fraud suggests that such fraud is widespread. Its reduction would be a major means of increasing the usable funds for public works projects. Any fraud or substandard construction is too much.

The problems include: (1) pay-offs, price-fixing, and influence peddling in the pre-construction stage; and (2) defective work, exhorbitant costs and extortion in the construction stage.

PRE-CONSTRUCTION FRAUD There are many kinds of illegal practices involved in zoning, land purchases, architectural/engineering awards, and construction contracts. In 1980 the Justice Department obtained indictments against 34 companies and 41 individuals in four states for conspiring to raise prices and allocate highway construction contracts. That investigation is continuing in other states.

Awards of architectural/engineering contracts on the basis of "contributions" to political parties is virtually institutionalized in many states and communities. The *Tennessee Journal* reports that architects and engineers seeking state business have known for decades that professional competence is not enough: political acceptability—as gauged by money contributions for gubernatorial and legislative races—is also required.[1]

In Massachusetts, the corruption commission found several instances of architectural firms generating substantial "political" funds from corporate monies—even though such corporate contributions have been illegal since 1946.

When firms "buy the job" through political contribution, the public can have little expectation that either the best firm has been chosen or that the public interest will be paramount in the subsequent construction. Such practices need not exist. Upon becoming Governor of Tennessee in 1979, Lamar Alexander reformed the process selection for architects and engineers used in state projects. By adapting selection guidelines prepared by the American Institute of Architects, a board chosen from professional organizations makes recommendations for the selection of architects and engineers. The state has also begun providing a public notification of proposed state construction projects. Previously, firms learned of potential projects from individuals and the relevant agencies on an ad hoc basis. The Commonwealth of Massachusetts is adopting major reforms in management of its public works expenditures, including creation of an independent inspector general.

CONSTRUCTION FRAUD AND POOR CONSTRUCTION   Fraudulent construction practices inflate project costs or result in deficient construction or both. A blue ribbon panel investigating bribery and corruption in award of public construction contracts in Massachusetts recently reported that over $6.4 billion of state and county building construction in the period 1968-1980 is defective, requiring repairs costing more than $2.1 billion (over $857 per Massachusetts resident).[2] The panel cited a variety of examples of defective work: At the University of Massachusetts, a toilet fell through a new, poorly-constructed floor when a student sat on it; an incompleted parking garage in Haverhill is already falling down, prompting local residents to demand its demolition; in Worcester, the county jail was built with cells that don't lock.[3] Although more than 60 percent of the state and county building work in Massachusetts in the period 1968-1980 was defective, such a high rate is probably not the norm for the nation as a whole. Corruption exists because of the lack of oversight by public agencies or collusion by responsible public officials.

Although the nation badly needs additional funding for public works projects, it will be difficult to secure voter approval for such funds if fraudulent activities are widespread and reform efforts are few. Thus, a prerequisite to national, state, and local efforts to build or rehabilitate essential public infrastructure is the elimination of fraud.

It will not be easy. The continued identification and prosecution of firms and individuals that engage in fraudulent activities are a minimal step. Indeed, a comprehensive review of the adequacy of present federal and state justice activities as to level and focus of effort is clearly needed. Resources put into such investigations will undoubtedly be cost effective in terms of reducing fraud.

Other measures should be taken to preclude the *opportunity* for many corrupt practices. The following actions would be a good beginning:

1. Standards for construction of various types of public works projects are required. Since the federal government supplies almost one-half of the funds for the nation's public works projects, and thus has the largest vested interest in preventing fraud, it should take the

lead in involving state and local government units, professional associations, and the construction industry in designing and applying such a set of standards. (In some public works areas, such standards already exist.) Such standards are necessary to provide an analytical framework for architectural/engineering design competition, funding decisions, and construction contract awards.

2. Public notification should become a standard procedure for *all* public works design, engineering, and construction contracts. Ad hoc notification approaches create the climate for fraud and favoritism.

3. Multiple oversight of public works activities is required. Such oversight should include funding agencies, independent inspector generals and local, state, and national legislative bodies. Perhaps the best and most easily replicable example of effective agency oversight of public works projects is found in the Economic Development Administration's public works program. Since its inception in 1965, that agency has had *no* scandal due to fraudulent public works design, engineering, or construction practices with its regular programs. At the same time EDA is a very small federal agency with total staffing of less than 1,000 persons. Its success is due to the following procedures:

a. The agency permits the recipients of its funds to use up to six percent of project funds to employ private architects and engineers. EDA engineers perform expert reviews of all projects at all stages.

b. At the pre-funding state, EDA engineers review proposed plans and cost estimates. If costs or designs are unreasonable, the project is rejected.

c. After a project is funded, the EDA Construction Review Division gives the community and architects/engineers a specific procedure to follow that includes competitive bidding for construction and ongoong detailing of expenses. EDA delegates to the private architects/ engineers construction oversight responsibility. However, at regular intervals, EDA engineers do full and partial review inspections of work *on-site,* and EDA staff commonly attend sessions when the principal competitive bids are opened.

The EDA procedures are both effective and efficient. Moreover, they are popular with project recipients and with architects and engineers because they are clear and equitably enforced.

In addition to oversight by agencies, increased Congressional oversight of fraudulent practices is needed.

4. Warranties on work are required. In addition to prosecuting individuals and firms that abuse the public through shoddy work, the public needs the assurance that defective projects will be replaced at little or no public cost. The $2.1 billion cost of repairing shoddy work in Massachusetts indicates the need for substantial warranties on public construction. Moreover, warranties are worthless unless enforced. Procedures are required for explicit and public waiving of warranty by public officials when they are *not* to be exercised.

58

A side benefit of design, engineering, and construction warranties will be reviews of firms and practices by insurance firms (much as they now do in private construction activities). While warranties may add a small amount to project costs, in the long term they will be a major deterrent to fraud and thus ultimately inexpensive. Certainly the people of Massachusetts would be better off today if their many defective projects had been covered with warranty insurance.

5. Standards are required to hold public officials *personally* accountable for their oversight of public works projects. Such accountability should include *financial* responsibilities for inadequate oversight and related derelictions of duties. Public officials can best be expected to put their heart into meeting their oversight responsibilities when they are personally liable for any incompetence or corruption associated with their work.

6. In Massachusetts the creation of a state corruption commission provided a mechanism for identifying and analyzing fraudulent practices that required reform. A similar *national* effort is required. Because of the prevalence of fraudulent public works activities and the need to reduce such abuses, a temporary Federal Commission of Public Works Design and Contracting should be established by the President and the Congress to identify specific actions necessary to reduce fraudulent public works activities.

WASTEFUL PROGRAM ADMINISTRATION Present administrative practices for public works are wasteful. There is no coherent approach to public works policy in the Executive Branch of the federal government. Policy setting has been dominated by individual Congressional committees, each pursuing different and sometimes inconsistent goals.

The GAO reports that there are wide variations in the capital budgeting procedures used by the individual agencies. No standards now exist for federal programs. Fundamental information used to guide the nation's public works investments is either non-existent, incomplete, or incomparable. For many types of service provided by public works there are no uniform service standards. The nation has neither an inventory of its capital stock nor assessments of its conditions—basic information that is necessary to establish priorities for future public works investments, rehabilitation, maintenance, and operation—nor any basis for making such assessments. The three agencies of the federal government which do collect information about public works are located in the Department of Commerce, but use different definitions, different geographic boundaries for reports, and different time periods. This reflects both their differing uses of the data and the lack of focus brought to public works data collection (Table 15).

Table 15
Summary of Public Works Data Strengths and Weaknesses by Source

Source	Strengths	Weaknesses
Bureau of the Census Governments Division	Data are centrally compiled Comprehensive governmental coverage Distinction between PWI expenditure types Grouping by functional category Spatial detail on state and local PWI Comparability between revenues and expenditures	Absence of quality control measures Absence of spatial detail on Federal PWI Lack of functional detail for PWI below national level Imprecise functional definitions Missing linkage between governmental revenues and PWI Measurement in current dollars only Measurement on fiscal year basis Changes in functional detail over time Construction PWI is not value put-in-place Lack of a consistent time series on individual small local governments Use of obligations to measure Federal equipment PWI
Bureau of Economic Analysis	Data are centrally compiled Comprehensvie governmental coverage Distinction between PWI expenditure types Detailed functional breakdown at national level for state and local PWI Measurement on calendar year basis Measurement in both current and constant dollars Compatibility of PWI with national income and product accounts Construction measured as value put-in-place	Absence of quality control measures Lack of functional detail for Federal PWI Absence of spatial detail Missing linkage between governmental revenues and PWI Exclusion of land purchases Use of obligations to measure Federal equipment PWI

Table 15 (Continued)
Summary of Public Works Data Strengths and Weaknesses by Source

Source	Strengths	Weaknesses
Federal Information Exchange System	Data are centrally compiled Consistent with OMB reporting procedures Conducive to analysis by • Function • Location • Type of Assistance • Agency	Federal obligation data only PWI not separately identified Absence of quality control measures Measurement in current dollars only Measurement on fiscal year basis Reliability of data below state level Changes in functional classifications over time
Independent Surveys: a. On-Site Visits	Precision control over data collection and management Linkage between revenues and PWI expenditures Identification of maintenance and renovation expenditures	Limited spatial coverage Measurement in current dollars Measurement on fiscal year basis
b. Mail/Phone Surveys	Precision control over data collection and management Spatial and temporal coverage	Limited agency coverage Incomparability between different types of outlays Measurement in current dollars Measurement on fiscal year basis

SOURCE: U.S. Department of Commerce, *A Study of Public Works Investment in the United States,* Washington, D.C., 1980.

Senator Robert Stafford of Vermont has declared federal policies on the construction, leasing, alteration and repair of government buildings that house federal workers to be in such an advanced state of disarray that they are actually "attracting confusion and influence, if not exorbitant waste; favoritism and scandal."[4]

Two examples illustrate Senator Stafford's point: (1) Present federal lease practices permit private entrepreneurs, often at virtually no risk, to finance, construct, and lease to the government for up to 20 years buildings having useful lives far in excess of these lease periods. Yet at the end of these leases, the entrepreneur owns the building and, as Senator Patrick Moynihan has commented, "the government is left with a stack of rent receipts." During the past decade, this practice has expanded—federal office space under lease has increased 117 percent to over 102 million square feet, and the amount of government-owned space under the management of the General Service Administration (GSA) has declined.[5] (2) A major portion of the GSA lease obligations are not reported in any budget. For example, the budget submitted to the Congress by the President in January 1980 requested $112 million in budget authority for GSA to make or renew leases on buildings. Upon investigation, the State Committee on Environment and Public Works determined that approval of this request would actually obligate the government to rental payments of approximately $1.03 billion during the fiscal year 1981 and the succeeding years of these lease commitments. This "omission" of $925 million of future obligations is altogether unreported anywhere—neither in the regular budget nor elsewhere "off-budget."[6] Although billions of dollars of federal funds are involved, the aggregate amount of GSA lease obligations from commitments of prior years remains unreported in the budget process. Reform of these practices has been a major agenda item of this Senate Committee, but obstacles have delayed progress.

There is also an absence of policy and administrative coherence for the annual $40 billion plus of public works assistance the federal government provides to state and local governments as well. Single-year funding and divergent criteria for the financing of similar types of facilities among the many federal funding agencies imposes major burdens on recipient state and local governments. For example, state and local capital budgeting is made dependent on annual changes in priorities, commitments, and funds from federal sources; excessive administrative obstacles are created in the use of federal funds; bureaucratic rigidity prevents the pooling of scarce public resources from several federal agencies to finance common projects; and, often there are duplications in some projects, while in other cases critical national and local projects are omitted.

For example, the federal financing of public works is heavily biased towards new construction. Many federal programs do not permit the use of funds for maintenance and rehabilitation. This bias induced many communities that are dependent on federal financing to forego maintenance and rehabilitation of basic facilities. Consequently, many existing public works facilities are allowed to deteriorate when limited funds for rehabilitation could restore them at a substantially lower cost than required for new construction. For example, the General Accounting Office reports that the old cast iron water mains in many cities could often be restored to an almost "new" condition through in-place scraping and relining at a cost between 30 and 50 percent of replacement expense.[7] In many cases not restoring these facilities results in wasting past investments that could be salvaged at less cost than new expenditures.

Attempted   Many studies have documented the ad-
Management Reform   ministrative confusion, excessive bur-
                                      dens, impediments to private sector
investments, barriers to the use of multiple financing sources, and lack
of priority-setting procedures in a variety of public programs, including those involving public works expenditures.

Efforts have been made to correct these deficiencies—reorganization; introduction of planning requirements; interagency task forces
and interagency cooperation agreements (such as the Under-
Secretaries and Assistant Secretaries Working Groups); centrally
directed program simplification efforts; A-95; intergovernment review
processes; and legislative coordination. Almost all have failed.

Reorganization and Public Works—One of the most attractive,
most often attempted, and least successful options to bring policy and
administrative coherence to the functions of government—including
public works—have been efforts to reorganize. Since 1948, there have
been 28 *major* but unsuccessful attempts to restructure and consolidate
federal economic policymaking—now delegated to 33 separate
departments and agencies *outside* the Executive Office of the
President.[8] None were successful.

Salamon suggests that reorganization is nothing more than the
continuation of politics by other means.[9] Reorganization for economy
or efficiency is rarely successful—the sums saved are often small in
comparison to the cost of the effort; increased efficiencies are either
miniscule or impossible to measure; and those savings which are
achieved generally come from programmatic changes that could have
been made without reorganization in the first place, rather than from
the reorganization itself. Efforts to achieve policy effectiveness
through reorganization always seem to slowly wind up concentrating
on institutional fragmentation as the primary impediment to coherent
policymaking—which it rarely is. Salamon concludes that most
reorganizations are used to:

> downgrade or get rid of an unwelcome official, to secure a change in
> Congressional venue, to bury a program, to change an agency's image,
> to give the appearance of action, to convey an impression of managerial
> confidence, to pay off a political debt, to forestall more radical change,
> to remove an agency from the budget or put it in, to shield an activity
> from congressional scrutiny or gain access, representation, visibility,
> and a secure institutional niche for a particular interest.

Interagency Coordination—Federal administrators have frequently
resorted to the use of working groups composed of senior officials
(career and appointed) representing various agencies involved in
common or shared responsibilities as a means of solving policy and
operational problems and "negotiating" working arrangements. Such
groups have included the Under-Secretaries Groups, Assistant

Secretaries Councils and other special purpose task forces. Recent efforts include the 1978 Urban Policy; the 1979 Rural Policy; and the 1980 Economic Renewal Policy.

Such approaches consume time and often substitute form for substance; are "fragile" because of the ascendancy of personal influence over such substantive matters as budgeting or policy objectives; and are operationally ineffective, for they generally fail to include regional, state, and local federal offices in policy, planning or budgetary decisions. Even when effective such relevance is generally short-lived because personalities that make such approaches work often change.

Program Simplification—There have been many attempts to simplify the administration of federal programs, including the block grant approach. Yet, considerable divisiveness and duplication exist even in those programs which have been "simplified." The Joint Funding Simplification Act of 1974 (Public Law 93-510) provided means for several federal agencies, state and local governments, and private (or even non-profit) organizations to negotiate and operate programs under a single formal and binding agreement that simultaneously committed several agencies to a common program of work.

However, during the period 1974-1978 the Act was used only 10 times. OMB, in an analysis of the Act, concluded that the Joint Simplification Act was not successful because: (1) federal agencies were not committed to using joint fundings and often refused to relate their own programs to common objectives; (2) there was a widespread ignorance of the Act and few persons knew how to use it at either federal, state, or local levels of government; (3) since the Act was permissive, many federal agencies ignored it; and (4) OMB itself had not provided adequate or timely leadership, support or oversight to assure implementation of the Act by federal agencies.[10]

Another attempt at simplification of federal requirements, the Rural Facilities Simplification Process, adopted in 1978, attempted to consolidate many of the federal administrative and application procedures that small, non-metropolitan communities must follow to secure funds from various federal programs. This effort, unlike many others, has successfully reduced and simplified many of the application requisites for joint projects and for determining which of several agencies will accept responsibility for a particular project. To date, however, concentration has been in pre-funding phases of projects and little attention has been given to simplifying and accelerating construction of projects once funding has been made.

The Intergovernmental Review and Comment Process—More than 200 federal programs now require that individual projects be reviewed by the concerned State and areawide planning institutions before sponsoring federal agencies will fund them. While this regulation has

64

been beneficial as an information exchange, it has done nothing either to reduce duplication among federal and state programs or to standardize multiple planning and administrative requirements. Also, the federal government is frequently unresponsive to negative reviews of projects, effectively discouraging substantive comments. If this program is to be effective, even as an information exchange, a number of improvements are needed, including: full compliance by federal agencies; improved cooperation among areawide planning bodies; clearer and more timely information about projects and their impacts; more funding for the A-95 clearinghouses; better training for A-95 staff; and a substantial reduction in paperwork involved in the A-95 process.

Convening Authorities—Another attempt to bring policy and program focus has been the use of convening and coordination authorities; the Congress and a succession of Presidents have passed legislation and issued Executive Orders giving Presidential appointees the "right" to call meetings with their peers to coordinate their mutual actions. Specifically, the Department of Housing and Urban Development has been given the authority to call meetings of the federal agencies engaged in urban development; the Department of Commerce has such authority for multi-state or regional development; and the Department of Agriculture has such authority for rural development. Upon closer examination, however, these authorities are meaningless. They only authorize the agency officials to call meetings—a prerogative they had without legislation. More importantly, these agencies are not empowered to enforce decisions.

Planning and Public Works—During the past two decades, there has been an increasing reliance on planning programs financed by the federal government but conducted by state or local institutions. In 1978, the Advisory Commission on Intergovernmental Relations (ACIR) inventoried federally sponsored planning programs.[11] The ACIR found:

■ There are 40 federal planning assistance programs in the fields of economic and community development; environmental protection; transportation; energy development; social services; public safety; and general policy development and management;

■ Federal planning requirements are now attached to approximately 150 federal aid programs.

The net effect of most federal planning programs is to impose on state, regional and local agencies duplication, disorder, and discord. As a result, most public planning is done chiefly to meet federal regulatory requirements or to secure federal funds. Planning requirements per se have proven to be neither an effective means of coordinating various federal programs, nor an effective link between federal, state and local management because: (1) The federal and state grants-in-aid programs operate separately without overall specific goals or objectives. Accordingly, agencies define their goals and objectives in terms of parochial, political, bureaucratic, and ideological considerations which often reflect agency wishes rather than the need of the public. (2) Virtually no attempts are made in planning to focus the many functional programs that may exist in a particular public works arena, such as water treatment, where there are seven district federal programs operating independently of each other. (3) Planning does not take into account the often disruptive, significant side effects and unintended consequences which result in the long term.

All of these efforts by Congress and the Executive Branch were attempts to achieve rationality and coordination among federal programs that do similar or related things in the same places. They were not sufficient to overcome the core problem that federal public works policy is made in a disjointed way by many individuals in many agencies and many legislative committees.

All of the tools were "band aids." The time has come for a more sweeping and difficult approach but one that has some chance of success—a capital budget.

FOOTNOTES TO CHAPTER 5

1. Smith, M. Lee, a series of articles in the period 1977–1980 on abuses in the use of architect-engineer contracts. The Tennessee Journal, Nashville, Tennessee.

2. State of Massachusetts, *Report of the Special Commission Concerning State and County Buildings,* Boston, Massachusetts, December, 1980.

3. Karagianis, Maria, "Defects: A Sad Slapstick Tale," The Boston Globe, Boston, Massachusetts, January 1, 1981.

4. Stafford, Robert, *Report to the Senate on Several Public Building Proposals,* Submitted by the General Services Administration, Committee on Environment and Public Works, United States Senate, Ninety-Fifth Congress, Second Session, Washington, D.C., 1978, p. 14.

5. Committee on Environment and Public Works, United States Senate, Ninety-Sixth Congress, Second Session, *Report to the Senate Committee on the Budget,* Washington, D.C., 1980, pp. 31–32.

6. Ibid.

7. *Additional Federal Aid for Urban Water Distribution Systems Should Wait Until Needs are Clearly Established,* GAO, pp. 8–19.

8. Office of Management and Budget, Executive Office of the President, "An unpublished report prepared for the President's Reorganization Project," Washington, D.C., 1978.

9. Salamon, Lester M., "In Pursuit of Reorganization: the Question of Goals," a paper delivered at the Administration Conference of the United States, Washington, D.C., 1980.

10. Office of Management and Budget, Executive Office of the President, *Report to Congress, Implementation of the Joint Funding Simplification Act of 1974 (Public Law 93-510),* Washington, D.C., February, 1979.

11. The White House Conference on Balanced National Growth and Economic Development, *Proceedings,* Washington, D.C., 1978.

6

A CAPITAL BUDGET FOR THE UNITED STATES

The federal, state and local governments have long used budgets as a device for bringing policy and administrative coherence to their operations. Virtually all major corporations, all state governments, and most local governments use capital budgets as basic policy and administration tools. Some states such as Pennsylvania and some cities such as Cincinatti, Ohio now include life-cycle costing in their capital budgets.

A major flaw in federal public works policymaking and program administration is the absence of national public works investment policies and a supporting capital budget.

This omission is no accident. It is the consequence of explicit decisions not to have a capital budget. It is explained in the *Special Analysis: Budget of the United States Government—1981* as follows:

> The Federal Government has never produced a capital budget in the sense of one in which capital or investment-type programs are financed separately from current expenditures. One major reason is that a capital budget could be misleading as a measure of the government's effect on the demand for economic resources. Another is that such a budget might favor programs with intensive expenditures for physical assets, such as construction, relative to other programs for which future benefits cannot be accurately capitalized, such as education or research. Likewise, physical assets might be favored relative to current operations in any given program, since deficit financing for capital would be easier to justify. A capital budget would also pose formidable accounting problems involving the measurement of depreciation on government property—[and] there are also inevitable classification difficulties.[1]

The annual Federal Budget of the United States submitted to the Congress each year presently contains three fundamental components: (1) the basic budget in overview; (2) a detailed budget appendix; (3) the special analyses. The special analyses are designed to highlight specified program areas or provide other significant presentations of federal budget data. These special analyses help bring policy and administrative overviews to 12 areas of major federal concern.

The preparation of one of these analyses, the special budget analysis of federal credit programs, demonstrates how useful a comprehensive annual accounting of fragmented federal activities can be. The federal government is engaged in numerous credit activities, including financing housing, rural electrification, support of rail programs, and the Export-Import Bank among others. These credit activities have major effects in both national and world credit markets. However, the assessment of these impacts was not possible until a standardized classification and accounting system was created to provide an overview of: (1) direct loans from the federal government; (2) federal guarantees of private lending; and (3) lending by privately-owned government sponsored enterprises. Once this analysis was created, the magnitude of these credit activities became clear. For example, the aggregate value of the federal government's loan guarantees now exceeds $239 billion. In fiscal year 1980, the on-budget and off-budget direct loan activities of the federal government exceeded $50 billion.[2] With accurate data, OMB is now able to better manage federal credit activities.

A thirteenth special analysis is now needed. The creation of a national capital budget analysis would permit a similar overview of the federal government's capital expenditures and commitments. As with the annual Federal Credit Analysis, it would permit consideration of public works activities in light of other national needs such as funding for social programs or for defense. It would also permit construction, rehabilitation, maintenance, and operational requisites to be explicitly considered.

The technical success of OMB in annually creating 12 special and complex budget analyses demonstrates that OMB can surmount the accounting and classification problems which might arise in creating a national public works capital analysis and a national public capital budget.

The Congress has demonstrated concern about the need to bring structure and focus to the federal public works investments. For example, the House of Representatives' Public Works Committee in 1974 sponsored research and hearings resulting in a call for the creation of a National Public Works Investment Strategy.[3] In 1976, the Congress directed the Department of Commerce to prepare what eventually became the 1980 report, *A Study of Public Works Investment in the United States.* The Congress held hearings and ordered that the studies be conducted on the use of public works as a counter-cyclical device in both 1978 and 1980. In 1980 the Committee on Environment and Public Works introduced legislation to create a systematic Federal Public Buildings Policy.[4] Numerous other committees of the House and Senate have conducted hearings and have sponsored studies on the deterioration of the nation's public infrastructure.

The time has come to annually prepare a special capital analysis in the President's Annual Budget and to create a national public works capital budget.

ELEMENTS OF A CAPITAL BUDGET   A national capital budget would consist of three essential components: (1) current and projected capital needs and expenditures; (2) current and projected operation and maintenance needs and expenditures; and (3) sources of financing.

Capital Expenditures   The budget would identify capital investment needs and (1) proposed federal investment in facilities to be used by federal government; and (2) proposed federal grant-in-aid financing of public works for state and local governments. Priorities would be identified. Both current and future (perhaps up to ten years) investments would be identified. To be useful for policymaking and program management, this information would ideally be disaggregated in a variety of ways, including:

(1) A division of investments by types of facilities such as aggregate investment in transportation, water treatment facilities, flood control facilities, airports, etc. This would be further divided by region or state. These two types of classifications could be used to prepare priority lists for investment both by types of facilities and areas. Among other information required to make such decisions would be analysis of the condition of existing facilities, quality of services provided, projections of future demand and estimates of alternative future investment costs.

(2) The identification of proposed public works investments by individual federal agencies. This would permit analysis of the roles of agencies when more than one makes the same type of investment. (For example, seven federal agencies now invest in water treatment facilities, each using differing policy and administrative criteria).

(3) The breakdown of capital expenditures between new construction, rehabilitation, land purchases, purchase of existing buildings, etc. (Such a breakdown would permit an assessment of where existing programs favor new construction over rehabilitation, and would facilitate life-cycle costing).

(4) A distinction between economic development investments and those public works related to basic community services (for example, industrial parks versus creation of recreation facilities).

Operation and Maintenance Expenditures   A national capital budget would include projections of the funds needed for operation and maintenance of federally-financed public works—by program, by type of project, and by area. Capital stock create demands for operation and maintenance funds. To avoid deferring maintenance and to insure funds to operate essential facilities, a number of cities, such as Cincinatti, Ohio, and Waco, Texas, will not consider making new capital construction unless there is a long-term assurance of long-term operation and maintenance funds. Similar standards are necessary for facilities whose construction and rehabilitation are wholly or partially funded by the federal government.

Sources of Financing

A national capital budget would classify public works investments (i.e., construction, rehabilitation, maintenance, and operation) and identify the responsible level of government for financing both specific categories of public works projects (roads, water supply, etc.) and the specific activities associated with those projects (construction, rehabilitation, maintenance, and operation).

POLICY AND MANAGEMENT USES OF A NATIONAL CAPITAL BUDGET

A national capital budget could bring new coherence to public works policy-making and program management by providing a framework for legislative and administrative decisions.

A capital budget would permit public works policymaking and program administration to be considered within a consistent framework of topics and subtopics. It would permit a greater degree of simplicity, and would lend validity and significance to decisions. Among other issues a national capital budget would provide a framework for analyzing in a systematic manner:

1. The aggregate requirement for domestic non-defense public works investments in the face of such other pressing claims such as national defense and social programs.

2. The relationship of public works investments to national defense, social, and economic development objectives.

3. The impacts of government regulatory actions on public works investments and operations. For example, mandated investments to assist the handicapped on public transportation threaten to bankrupt some public transportation systems such as those in New York City.

4. The consequences of allocations of limited public works funds as between new construction, rehabilitation of existing facilities, and operation maintenance.

5. The social and equity issues associated with the distribution of public works funds among and between various regions.

6. The sources, consequences, and alternative financing sources of public works projects and their operation.

Capital budgeting is ultimately a political process through which resources are allocated to meet a variety of objectives. The creation of such a budget would provide a framework in which: (a) the advocates for federal investments in public works would negotiate these potential expenditures against other uses of federal funds such as national defense and education; (b) funds would be allocated among such programs as transportation, water treatment, and navigation, etc.; and (c) funds would be allocated among construction, operation, maintenance, and rehabilitation activities.

A capital budget would ultimately serve as a device by which the President and the Congress could bring necessary control to the present "free form" investment and management practices of the various federal public works agencies and permit effective Congressional management, especially of Congress's own committee actions which have been a major contribution to duplication and inconsistency.

Public works investments reflect a history of choices, decisions, bargains, compromises, and allocations which provide a foundation for present and future actions. A capital budget could chronicle this important set of information. It could also articulate a statement of the future, specifying goals and resources needed to attain those goals. States and communities, now dependent on federal public works funding, operate on a year-to-year basis with the ever present possibility that federal "commitments" will be altered or regulations changed. State and local governments need more certainty than a one-year federal budget. The private sector similarly would also profit from improved certainty. For example, the private sector could have adjusted more efficiently to ever-changing air and water control standards if in the early 1970s, the federal government had more clearly specified their intentions in this field.

The creation of any public facility places a variety of demands on other public programs and services. A national capital budget could provide a mechanism for identifying and quantifying these relationships.

Choosing Basic Goals and Objectives

Clearly stated goals and objectives for federal public works investments are required to give a common direction to policymaking and program investment.

These goals will necessarily be influenced by the availability of resources and must accord with other social, area development (urban, rural, and regional), sectoral, industrial, and macro-economic policies. Among goals which require specification are: (1) the basic levels of public works services to be provided for specific populations and specific geographic areas; and (2) the extent the public sector will finance infrastructure to support economic development.

Once these and other goals have been articulated, they can serve as the basis for motivating the bureaucracy (thus creating a sound management control system), providing a realistic framework within which programs can be evaluated and, a solid foundation for creating a public works management philosophy relevant to the needs and political/financial realities of the 1980s.

Research, Analytical Evaluation, and Data Requirements   Although all levels of government have long made substantial annual investments in public works, there has been an amazingly small amount of research and analysis on the topic. Thus, many significant information gaps exist, including:

■ *Data.* Data on public works are fragmented and often incomparable among the various data series. There is no inventory of the nation's capital stock, virtually no estimate of the condition of individual facilities or the quality of service they provide, no estimate of future capital needs, and no estimate of the funds that will be required to maintain and operate existing and proposed facilities. Limited data exist on the fiscal capacities of governments to finance these expenditures.

■ *Replacement/Repair.* There are no standardized replacement/repair analytical techniques—techniques which systematically determine when it is economically feasible to replace or repair facilities.

■ *Demographics.* There are virtually no analyses of the role of public works in stimulating shifts in population and economic activity among and between regions of the nation.

■ *Counter-cyclical Spending.* The studies on the use of counter-cyclical public works have been limited to temporary programs. Virtually no attention has been given to the use of the nation's $80 billion of annual public works investments as a major tool for economic stabilization.

■ *New Technology.* There are only limited analyses of how new techniques can be implemented to extend the life of existing facilities or how to provide the same service in a better, less expensive way.

■ *Financing.* The alternative financing of future public works investments has received little attention, and has focused only on the introduction of limited purpose tools such as national urban banks or selected application of user charges. There has been no overall analysis of the impact of future financing requirements on capital markets in general or on available alternatives.

■ *Operational Data.* Operational data necessary for managing programs, such as temporary public works, either do not exist or are inadequate.

■ *Funded Projects.* Information on the status of projects already funded but not yet constructed is not collected in a systematic manner. This oversight has contributed to the creation of the $100 billion backlog of funded but uncompleted public works projects.

73

■ *Evaluation.* No systematic system for evaluating the nation's public works policies or programs exists.

Financing

A basic function of a national public works capital budget is the identification of sources and uses of financing. The creation of such a new policy tool will necessarily involve a complete review of present and future financing options, including, federal, state and local fiscal capabilities.

Personnel Policies

The recent studies on public works investments have consistently excluded personnel considerations. Yet, a major cause of the rapid deterioration of many public works facilities is inadequately trained personnel. Thus, a major element in the creation of a national public works investment strategy or a national budget is the identification of personnel needs and an assessment of the efficacy of present recruitment and training procedures. For example, the federal government must seriously consider whether or not it should make capital investments when communities cannot demonstrate that they will have well-trained personnel to operate these facilities.

A second personnel consideration involves federal managers. Presently, the federal agencies rarely school even senior managers in the logic and techniques of strategic management. If a national capital budget is to be created, training programs in these techniques of strategic management are essential for participants. (Private firms such as IBM, General Electric, and Control Data regularly invest substantial funds in training even the most senior management in strategic management techniques. The federal government should do no less).

A third personnel improvement that is required is training of federal, state and local officials in the techniques and economics of real estate and public works development and management. Given the quantities of public funds involved, and the impact of these funds on the quality of life of the nation and its cities, their physical structure and economic development, such training should be a basic requisite for individual employment and advancement. Given the large numbers of officials now in position of responsibility who have not had such training, remedial courses should be made mandatory—starting with the most senior officials *first*.

REQUISITES FOR SUCCESSFUL CREATION OF A NATIONAL CAPITAL BUDGET

Many attempts have been made to bring policy and program coherence to the operations of government through budgeting, such as Zero-Based Budgeting (ZBB) and Planning, Programming, and Budgeting Systems (PPBS). However, such approaches to improved decisionmaking have most often failed because of: (1) the complexity of the systems themselves; (2) internal resistances to change; and (3) the manner in which these systems were introduced. Perhaps most importantly, these systems failed because the budget instrument itself was seen as the mechanism for change rather than the result of a larger, overall process of policy and administrative reform.

If a national capital budget is to be created and successfully used as a policy and management tool, a number of conditions are necessary. Steiner identifies a number of those needed elements for successful budgeting in the private sector.[5] Slightly modified they are equally, if not more, applicable to capital budgeting in the public sector:

■ The leadership of the President and Congressional support are essential, particularly in the early stages.

■ The budget process must cover all the federally financed public works activities—construction, rehabilitation, operation, maintenance, and financing.

■ The budget process must be directly tied to the planning process overall and for specific programs. Although the budget is not the only planning process, it is the major device for formalizing plans and translating them into operations. This linkage must be recognized and accommodated.

■ The responsibility for creating and operating the national capital budget must be clearly assigned. This assignment will define who is expected to do what, by when, and what standards are to be met. In the Executive Branch there is only one logical choice for administering the national capital budget—the Office of Management and Budget. The Office of Management and Budget has overall budgeting responsibilities; the expertise necessary to prepare a national capital budget; and the power necessary to integrate this budget with other claims on resources.

■ As with the Executive Branch, the responsibility for capital budgeting should be assigned to a specific committee of the Congress. Among other logical choices are the public works committees and the budget committees. Irrespective of which committee is given such a responsibility, the Congressional Budget Office should prepare a special annual analysis of the federal government's long- and short-term capital investments.

■ The capital budget should contain a degree of flexibility. Circumstances change and fixed budgets will at times require modification to accommodate these changes. The knowledge that unusual circumstances can be accommodated will permit the creation of a capital budgeting process responsive to both anticipated and unanticipated needs—a basic requisite for effective management and on-going support from those involved in the budgeting process.

■ The language of capital budgeting must be kept as free of complex accounting terms as possible. One of the present difficulties with the various public budgets is the use of "jargon." What may be "state-of-the-art" terminology to budgeteers confuses policymakers and others who are essential to creating and carrying out an effective budgetary process. Thus, a common terminology should be uniformly applied; this will permit communication not now possible.

■ The budgeting system itself should be kept as simple as possible. As Steiner points out, "Budgets are tools for management, not management itself . . . too much complexity and restriction will create frustration, then resentment and finally inertia."

■ Capital budgets must have clear standards upon which performance will be based and evaluated. Such standards must be fair, clear, and firmly applied.

■ The final and most important requisite is the initial and on-going participation of principals—at both policy and operational levels—in the budget process. Although there are limits to such participation, the degree of support for the capital budget process will generally rise proportionately to the degree of participation. Such participation will permit the identification of problems that often go unnoticed until remedial action is required. A capital budget can be a basic tool for creating an overall design for policies and actions. It is not a punitive device for frustrating the functions of an organization. Nor can it in itself serve as a means to good performance. Other management tools are available for purposes of incentive.

This budget could serve as an initial guide for coordinating federal actions with those of state and local governments. It would necessarily represent the culmination of an intensive and close interaction between the Executive Branch and the Congress, with state and local governments, and with the private sector.

The nation needs clearer definitions about which level of government is accountable for what. Present confusion within the system accounts for much of the existing waste and the deterioration in our public works.

FOOTNOTES TO CHAPTER 6

1. Office of Management and Budget, Executive Office of the President, *Special Analyses: Budget of the United States,* Washington, D.C., January, 1980, p. 91.

2. *Special Analyses: Budget of the United States,* pp. 141–207.

3. Committee on Public Works, U.S. House of Representatives, *A National Public Works Investment Policy,* Ninety-Third Congress of the United States, Second Session, Washington, D.C., December, 1974.

4. United States Senate, Ninety-Sixth Congress, Second Session, S.2080 "Public Buildings Act of 1980," Washington, D.C., 1980.

5. Steiner, George A., *Top Management Planning,* Macmillan Publishing Company, New York City, New York, 1969.

7

ALLOCATING PUBLIC WORKS RESPONSIBILITIES WITHIN THE FEDERAL SYSTEM

Since every dollar must count in the 1980s, it does behoove us to re-examine and reallocate public works responsibilities and authorities among the various levels of government. Over the past 20 years, with the enthusiastic support of most state and local governments, the role of the federal government in financing local public works has steadily increased. In 1957, the federal government funded ten percent of state and local public works investments; by the late 1970s, over 40 percent of these expenditures were federally financed.[1] Today, funding from federal appropriations has eclipsed state and local debt financing as the primary source of investment in state and local public facilities.

DILUTED ACCOUNTABILITY An assessment of what level of government should be responsible for financing each type of public facility would go to the heart of the complex and frequently duplicative network of inter-governmental relationships that has evolved since the Second World War. In the decade of economic and fiscal constraints that lies ahead, it may prove necessary to simplify these relationships in order to ensure that accountability at each level of government for the responsibilities allocated to it are consistent with its fiscal, territorial, and statutory capacities.

There are at least 100 separate federal agencies, 50 state governments, (each with their separate agencies), the District of Columbia, Puerto Rico, the protectorates, 3,042 counties, 35,000 general purpose local governments, 15,000 school districts, 2,000 areawide units of government, over 200 interstate compacts, and nine multi-state regional development organizations all engaged in public works planning and construction.[2] Although responsibilities and authorities within these governments are intertwined, neither their public works policy-making nor their administration reflect a coherent focus. Indeed, they are often engaged in fierce competition for resources and bureaucratic turf—a competition which too often results in an actual reduction of effort and increased waste.

Equally significant, their relationships are vertical. Highway agencies at each level are closely linked. So, too, are water and

78

sewerage agencies, community development organizations, etc. These vertical alliances of functional agencies are the heart of the new "Administration State." But there are no politically-accountable horizontal decisionmaking and planning institutions that cross-cut these vertical kingdoms in the Administrative State to ensure that their separate actions add up to coherent results over-all. It is too much to expect that the President, a Governor, a Mayor, or a County Commissioner can surmount the vertical fragmentation that has been generalized over the last three decades.

The existing fragmentation creates a number of bureaucratic perversions, including: the loss of accountability for the elected officials of general government; limited pooling of public resources; duplication of some facilities and services and the omission of others; contradictory and redundant activities and conflicting program procedures; divergent delivery systems and eligibility criteria; and a lack of clarity as to the assignment of specific authorities and responsibilities for financing construction, rehabilitation, maintenance and operation.[3] The policy and program disorders which have resulted greatly exceed the planning and administrative capacities of the federal, state and local governments to correct without fundamental changes.

Fragmentation is not solely the product of special interests or bureaucratic expansionism; it also mirrors the fragmentation which inevitably results when Congress is heavily dependent upon the work of its Committees to produce legislation. Recent budget reforms in Congress have provided the basis for horizontal, cross-cutting procedures by means of which Congressional leadership can judge proposed legislative initiatives against the back-drop of statutes already on the books and proposals emerging from other standing committees. But the potential of the new budget process to promote legislative coherence is yet to be fully realized. As a consequence, executive agencies are all too often blamed for duplication and conflict that is not really their own doing, but is the result of fragmentation on the legislative process itself. At present, national capital budgeting, coupled with the Congressional Budget reforms, offers a practical and effective means to confront much of the present fragmentation.

ALLOCATION OF POWERS AND FUNCTIONS

No clear allocation of responsibilities and functions exists among and between the various levels of government. Prior to the 1960s, the division of powers and functions between national and state governments for provision of public works activities was relatively definable.

The federal government funded and operated projects that were in the national interest and were beyond the fiscal capacities of the states and private sector—projects such as flood control and navigation on the Mississippi River. Such federal aid to state and local governments as did exist, as in aid for highway construction, was based on the premise of partnership in which each partner put up approximately half of the funds. The assumption was that the facilities being built served both national and local needs.

However, as James Sundquist, of the Brookings Institution has noted, the early 1960s brought a distinct change in the evolution of American federalism.[4] The national government aggressively embarked on a course of using state and local governments as vehicles to achieve federally-defined national objectives. The categorical grant assistance programs became the most influential tools the federal government could use to pursue this new activist role. To induce state and local participation, matching requirements were lowered or even eliminated. Close federal administrative control was introduced and numerous projects were funded on an individual basis with decisions centralized in Washington. The fundamentals of American federalism were altered. Recipients of aid often dealt directly with federal agencies. State and local policymakers were designed out of the system. Indeed, in some programs, federal funds were provided to recipients to enable them to face city hall and the state house as adversaries. Non-profit organizations of many kinds were created to be recipients of federal funds in order to bypass local and state governments.

Continuing this trend toward centralism, regulation became an increasingly powerful tool used by the federal government to mandate state and local actions in the 1970s. While in 1969 there were fewer than 30 federal regulatory agencies, there were approximately 100 such agencies in 1980.[5] And during the 1970s, another departure was taken from the presumed principles of American federalism when the federal government began to impose general mandates upon state and local governments that were not tied to specific federal programs, but were imposed as general requirements that state and local governments were expected to meet without federal financial recompense. These included requirements such as providing full access to buildings and services for the handicapped, requirements that wages paid to workers on public projects be consistent with the Davis-Bacon Act, and requirements levied on all projects under a variety of environmental protection acts. Such general mandates effectively bypassed the legislative responsibilities of local and state governments. They "appropriated" state and local funds outside their legislative processes at either level.

There have been efforts over the past decade to address some of the problems resulting from this drift toward a more unitary or centralized system. Attempts have been made to consolidate many categorical programs into block grants to provide more state and local flexibility. Revenue-sharing went still further by untying grant requirements from the state and local use of federally-raised funds. These reforms have been partially effective. By 1980, 22 percent of the federal grants were either block grants or revenue sharing ($18.4 billion out of $82.9 billion). Nonetheless, over 78 percent of federal assistance still remains categorical.[6]

As useful as the creation of block grant and revenue sharing programs have been, they do not answer the question of who should be responsible for what within our federal system. Which types of public works should be the responsibility of the federal government? Which should be the responsibility of the state and local governments? Which should be a shared responsibility? Which types of financing, (construction, rehabilitation, maintenance and operation) should be the responsibilities of which levels of government? For example, if the federal government finances construction of sewerage treatment facilities, which level(s) of government should assume responsibility for maintenance and operational expenses and under what conditions? We cannot afford the redundancy and diluted accountability of our present system under the special financial constraints we will face in the 1980s.

The point was articulated by then Governor Ronald Reagan in 1972:

> Do we have the will and the courage to look at our government structure; to evolve a practical plan whereby tasks and services performed by the government will be assigned to those levels of government best qualified to handle them regardless of what has been the pattern of the past; to construct a revenue system that matches with sufficient tax resources the tasks assigned to each level of government?[7]

During the past two decades, as responsibilities for various governmental functions or components of functions have been shifted from one governmental unit to another, there have been a growing number of attempts to redefine appropriate functional responsibilities. The Advisory Commission on Intergovernmental Relations reports that most of these shifts have been vertical—between levels of government. The trend of these shifts has been to elevate responsibilities to higher levels of government reflecting: (1) the conclusion of many local leaders that many services can best be performed by larger units of government where economies of scale are possible; (2) the need to shift fiscal responsibilities to levels of government with a more productive fiscal base; and (3) the political attractiveness of using sources of financing for which local leaders are not responsible.

In the past two decades there has been an increase in the number of special interest groups (many of which are federally financed) that are skilled in bringing political pressure to bear on all levels of government. They have been successful in shifting emphasis to social and other programs at the sacrifice of public works activities. Even within the sphere of public works expenditures, special interest groups have been able to convince political leaders to allocate funds to specific types of projects and activities irrespective of their implications for the long-run viability of the national and regional economies.

The use of public works funding as a tool of power politics has been as American as cherry pie. At all levels, the extension or withholding of specific public works projects has always been used to entice or force decisions on other, often unrelated, issues. Public works policy has been almost entirely a Congressional prerogative since the founding of the Republic and federal public works projects have been the progeny of legislative "rough and tumble."

In an era of tight economic and financial constraints, when public works must be viewed as fundamental to the long-term health of the national economy and the provision of services essential to social stability, we can no longer afford the luxury of pork or special interest politics. We must construct at each level of government both executive and legislative procedures that imbue public works investment with the long-term perspectives required for a sound, long-range, carefully timed capital investment program.

IMPROVING ACCOUNTABILITY: REALLOCATING FUNCTIONS

In this bicentennial decade of our Constitution, it is singularly appropriate that we undertake a major assessment of the drift that has been occuring in our federal system and to redefine, in the context of the coming decades, the roles and responsibilities of each level of government. To the extent that some functions, such as welfare, can be nationalized, resources may be freed up at the state level to renovate and modernize infrastructure.

Such an assessment is beyond the scope of this book. It can be undertaken best by the Advisory Commission on Intergovernmental Relations or a new national commission created for the purpose.

But in the field of public works, several principles are worth setting forth:

1. *The level of government mandating a requirement must be prepared to pay for it.*

Mandated public works investments are a major source of the fiscal stress on state and local governments. The federal government has mandated a broad array of investments for state and local governments (at least 1,500), and state governments have imposed an equal or larger number on local governments. The fiscal and economic strains placed on state and local governments can be highly disruptive, forcing postponement of investment that may be vital in the long-run. To reduce the fiscal and economic strains on local governments, a reassessment of mandating by the federal and state governments is

82

essential. The ACIR has identified a number of steps for such an evalution:[8]

■   Inventory existing mandates;

■   A review procedure is needed to identify, eliminate, postpone, or alter unnecessary or overly restrictive mandates;

■   Create federal and policy statements and review procedures for all proposed mandates;

■   Full federal and state reimbursement for mandates that intrude into issues that are essentially state and local concerns, such as working hours and working conditions;

■   A procedural safeguard to insure an equitable and efficient reimbursement process.

2. *Functions that are in the national interest should not be imposed on inappropriate levels of jurisdiction lacking the capacity to deliver. To the extent that state and local jurisdictions are used as vessels of administrative convenience to meet a national need, the federal government must finance the cost from national tax revenues.*

3. *On the other hand, federal financing of public works should not supplant local or state responsibilities or capacities. It should be used to finance those necessary works clearly beyond the financial responsibilities and capacities of the jurisdictions involved.*

Existing grants-in-aid should be evaluated from a number of points of view.

a) Does a particular grant-in-aid promote capital substitution or is it too stimulative? The 50/50 matching ratio used in the federal highway programs of the past permitted states to construct roads then desired by the states and also met national needs. Given the political pressures that always exist with road construction, the states were almost without exception anxious to raise their 50 percent matching funds. Thus, a stimulative effect was created. When these ratios were increased to 70-90 percent, the relative stimulative impact was diminished and funding responsibilities and control increasingly passed to the federal government.

b) Is it intended to equalize capacity or simply underwrite operations? The choice of intentions or mix is important to any reform of the system. For example, revenue sharing is less unlikely to result in public works construction than either block grant programs or categorical assistance given these latter programs' restrictions. For example, GAO reports that in Fiscal Year 1977, only 1.2 percent of total General Revenue Sharing funds went to municipal water projects ($79 million of $6.55 billion), while 23 percent of EDA's $300 million were so allocated. Conversely, revenue sharing would more likely result in operation and maintenance expenditures than construction oriented categorical programs.

4. *Public works financing must promote the maintenance of the*

nation's infrastructure once built rather than focus solely on construction.

The prepondernance of federal programs fund new construction without concern for long-run maintenance and replacement. Future assistance should also focus on life-cycle costing and maintenance.

5. *Federal public works policy must accommodate the diversity of regional needs and problems and not impose rigidly standardized approaches irrelevant to the realities of national development.*

Sectionalism has long been a divisive force in American politics. the allocation of public works funds is politically sensitive. *At present, when all public works funds are considered, there is a fairly even per capita allocation between regions.*[10] The West and South receive more funds through the Corps of Engineers and the Bureau of Reclamation than the Northeast and Midwest, but industrial Midwest and Northeast receive more funds from other categorical public works programs.

Each region of the country faces quite different problems in meeting national economic objectives. Many Northeastern cities require funds for rehabilitation of obsolescent facilities. Many Southern and Western cities require funds for new construction. Rural regions such as the Great Plains and large areas of the Southwest face acute water problems that will affect the nation's agricultural and energy output.

The nation has a stake in resolving these development problems in all of its regions, for they serve as major impediments to national economic renewal.

6. *State and local governments must lessen their growing dependence on federal aid by reassuming responsibility for the financing and delivery of those functions which are clearly assigned to them in terms of their capacity, responsibility, and jurisdiction.*

The states are given a crucial role under the Constitution. They alone have the power to form the boundaries and define the functions of local units of government. They possess all the powers which were not explicitly extended to the national government through the Constitution. And, of course, they have the ability to revise their own constitutions at will. All of these powers have been used erratically. Through legislation and a series of constitutional amendments, the states have constrained their own ability to provide necessary public works through tax, borrowing and expenditure limitations. As a result, they have been forced to reduce essential services, abandon certain functions altogether, and to rely even more heavily on federal financing. Indeed, the increasing role played by the federal government in the construction of basic public works is as much the result of these self-inflicted federalist wounds as the aggressiveness of an ambitious national government.

Just as the national government must re-examine its own functions and responsibilities in light of the economic realities of the 1980s, so, too, must the state governments and thereby the local governments they have created.

Basic systems of local government functions, organization, and finance require fundamental assessment. To match the evaluation of appropriate federal functions, a reallocation of functions between the state and local governments will prove just as necessary. States may have to assume financial and operating responsibilities for certain facilities and services hitherto provided by municipalities. Counties may have to be granted legislative charters and some municipal responsibilities in order to encompass the patterns of economic and social life that have expanded beyond the reach of municipal boundaries.

Dependence upon the local property tax may have to be replaced by increased use of other, progressive taxes. While states ease fiscal restrictions on their local jurisdictions, they may have to assume increased responsibility for auditing and overseeing the financial integrity of their own jurisidictions.

But most important, states working closely with their local jurisdictions will find it essential to shift more of their resources toward investment in capital infrastructure. And in many states, that will require new approaches to state capital financing.

State governments and most municipal governments use capital budgeting, but in the overwhelming number of cases such budgeting represents the compilation of project listings from individual agencies rather than within an overall framework. Project management techniques in the public sector significantly lag behind those in the private sector construction.

Reform is needed in public works activities at all levels of government.

FOOTNOTES TO CHAPTER 7

1. *A Study of Public Works Investment in the United States.*

2. *Statistical Abstract,* p. 283.

3. Office of Management and Budget, Executive Office of the President, *Reorganization Study of Local Development Assistance Programs,* Washington, D.C., December, 1978.

4. Advisory Commission on Intergovernmental Relations, *Categorical Grants: Their Role and Design,* Washington, D.C., 1978, p. 31.

5. *Being Number One: Rebuilding the U.S. Economy.*

6. *Special Analyses: Budget of the United States Government,* Fiscal Year 1981, pp. 239–277.

7. Advisory Commission on Intergovernmental Relations, *State Planning of Local Expenditures*, Washington, D.C., July, 1978.

8. Ibid.

9. *Additional Federal Aid for Urban Water Distribution Systems Should Wait Until Needs are Clearly Established*, p. 38.

10. *A Study of Public Works Investment in the United States—Summary*.

8

RECOMMENDATIONS

At this critical juncture, when much of the nation's attention must be focused on economic renewal, can we find the resources needed to renovate, replace, or construct the public facilities needed to underpin the industrial economy? Can we institute the practices and procedures required to make the most effective use of whatever resources we have?

It is possible so long as we are not tempted to fall back upon ineffective tinkering. Wholesale revolution is not necessary either. But it does mean that the Executive Branch must share responsibility for creating and managing public works policy more coherently than in the past.

A NATIONAL CAPITAL BUDGET A systematic and orderly approach to public capital investment must replace the loose, give-and-take procedures of the legislative process we have known in the past.

(1) Congress should require the preparation of a *Special Analysis* to accompany each annual budget outlining the nation's public works needs as they affect national economic performance.

(2) Congress should direct the Executive Branch to undertake an inventory of national public works needs as they affect the economy.

(3) With the inventory as a starting point, Congress should then require preparation of a Capital Budget that proposes phased capital investments matched to both short-term cyclical and long-term national economic needs. The budget would display preconstruction, construction, maintenance, and operating costs.

(4) Congress should direct the Executive Branch to begin preparation of the required data bases required to make national capital budgeting feasible. The data systems should be designed to enable Congress and the Executive Branch to manage federal public works investments so that they are counter-cyclical rather than pro-cyclical. The systems should identify back-logged projects in the inventory, the construction of which can be accelerated when economic circumstances indicate.

The systems should also display:

■ Economic linkages—The linkages between specific types of public works construction and the purchase of related materials and employment. Such data are essential for targeting public works investments to specific economic sectors and work forces *outside* of on-site construction activities.

■ Improved Industrial Capacity Data—If public works purchases are to be made on a cyclical basis, better data must be prepared on utilization rates of key industries involved with public works construction and more detailed monthly capacity utilization data than are now available.

■ Data for Triggering Devices—The major weakness found by virtually every analysis of the LPW program was the inadequacy of unemployment and other data used in triggering decisions. Rather than patch together disparate and unsatisfactory data sources which result in an inadequate counter-cyclical public works triggering device, a more productive and less expensive course of action would be to create specific data series which meet specific triggering objectives.

MAKING THE PUBLIC WORKS DOLLAR GO FARTHER

(5) Congress should direct the Executive Branch to report by an appropriate date steps by means of which delays in public facilities construction can be reduced through reforms in federal, state, and local administrative procedures. Similar efforts in reducing other regulatory delays are already underway at the direction of the President.

(6) Congress and the Executive Branch should consider undertaking a series of reforms designed to minimize corruption and waste connected with public works expenditures.

(7) The Executive Branch should undertake an administrative evaluation of the scattered public works activities of the federal government and be prepared to consummate consolidated reforms simultaneously with the proposed Public Works Report to Congress.

CLARIFYING RESPONSIBILITIES

(8) Congress or the Executive Branch should direct the Advisory Commission on Intergovernment Relations or a new body constituted for the purpose to review the public works responsibilities of each level of government and propose appropriate guidelines for allocating functions and responsibilities.

CONCLUSION

It would be all too tempting to avoid the difficulties of disentangling the knotted threads of intergovernmental complexity and to assume that federal public works expenditures must be drastically curtailed in the face of current economic conditions. But such a course would contravene the very purposes of economic policy now being formulated.

Economic renewal must be the premier focus of domestic policy in this decade. Our public infrastructure is strategically bound-up in that renewal. Without attention to deterioration of that infrastructure, economic renewal will be thwarted if not impossible.

We have no recourse but to face the complex task at hand of rebuilding our public facilities as an essential prerequisite to economic renewal and maintenance of our quality-of-life.

BIBLIOGRAPHY

Abt Associates, Inc., *National Rural Community Facilities Assessment Study,* Boston, Massachusetts, 1980.

Advisory Commission on Intergovernment Relations, Washington, D.C.

1. A Catalog of Federal Grant-in-Aid Programs to State and Local Governments: Grants Funded FY 1975. (A-52a), October, 1977

2. *Improving Federal Grants Management.* (A-53), February, 1977.

3. *The Intergovernmental Grant System as Seen by Local, State, and Federal Officials.* (A-54). March, 1977.

4. *Community Development: The Workings of a Federal-Local Block Grant.* (A-57). March, 1977.

5. *The States and Intergovernmental Aids.* (A-59). February, 1977.

6. *Federal Grants: Their Effects on State-Local Expenditures, Employment Levels, and Wage Rates.* (A-61). February, 1977.

7. *The Intergovernmental Grant System: An Assessment and Proposed Policies.* (B-1). 1978.

8. *Restructuring Federal Assistance: The Consolidation Approach,* Bulletin No. 79-6. October 1979.

9. *Categorical Grants: Their Role and Design.* (A-52). May, 1977.

10. *Pragmatic Federalism: The Reassignment of Functional Responsibility.* July, 1976.

11. *State Involvement in Federal-Local Grant Programs.* (M-55).

12. *State Mandating of Local Expenditures.* (A-67). July, 1978.

13. *Measuring the Fiscal Capacity and Effort of State and Local Areas.* (M-58). March, 1971.

14. *Multistate Regionalism.* (A-39). April, 1972.

Aldrich, Mark, *A History of Public Works in the United States,* 1790-1970, U.S. Department of Commerce, Washington, D.C., 1979.

Alexander, Governor Lamar, *The Five Year Capital Budget for the State of Tennessee. 1980-81, 1984-85.* The Government of the State of Tennessee, Nashville, Tennessee, January, 1980.

91

American Public Works Association, *A History of Public Works in the United States,* Chicago, Illinois, 1976.

Anthony, Robert N., *Planning and Control Systems: A Framework for Analysis,* Harvard University, Boston, Massachusetts, 1965.

Bryce, Herrington, J., *Small Cities,* Lexington Books, Lexington, Massachusetts, 1979.

Centaur Associates, Inc. *Economic Development Administration Title I Public Works Program Evaluation,* Washington, D.C., May, 1979.

Chamber of Commerce of the United States, *Improving Local Government Fiscal Management: Action Guidelines for Business Executives.* Washington, D.C., 1979.

Choate, Pat, "As Time Goes By: The Costs and Consequences of Delay." The Academy for Contemporary Problems, Columbus, Ohio. 1980.

Choate, Pat, *The High Plains Project,* Economic Development Administration, Washington, D.C., March, 1978.

Choate, Pat, "Urban Revitalization and Industrial Policy: The Next Steps." Testimony before the Subcommittee on the City, Committee on Banking, Finance, and Urban Affairs, U.S. House of Representatives on hearings on Urban Revitalization and Industrial Policy. Washington, D.C., September 17, 1980.

Committee on Environment and Public Works, United States Senate, 95th Congress, 2nd Session. *Report to the Senate of Several Public Buildings Proposals,* Washington, D.C., August, 1978.

Committee on Environment and Public Works, United States Senate, 96th Congress, 1st Session. *Report to the Senate Committee on the Budget.* Washington, D.C., March, 1979.

Committee on Environment and Public Works, United States Senate, 96th Congress, 2nd Session. *Report to the Senate Committee on the Budget.* Washington, D.C., March, 1980.

Committee on Public Works, United States Senate, 93rd Congress, 2nd Session, *Construction Delays and Unemployment.* Washington, D.C., 1974.

Committee on Public Works of the U.S. House of Representatives, *A National Public Works Investment Policy,* Washington, D.C., December, 1974.

Congressional Budget Office of the U.S. Congress, *Countercyclical Uses of Federal Grant Programs,* Washington, D.C., November, 1978.

Congressional Research Service of the Library of Congress, *Review of Title V Commission Plans,* Washington, D.C., 1977.

Consad Research Corporation, *A Study of Public Works Investment in the United States,* published by the U.S. Department of Commerce, Washington, D.C., April, 1980.

Devoy, Robert and Wise, Harold, *The Capital Budget,* The Council of State Planning Agencies, Washington, D.C., 1979.

Due, John F. *Government Finance,* The Richard D. Irwin Company, Homewood, Illinois, 1959.

The Economic Development Administration of the U.S. Department of Commerce, *An Updated Evaluation of the EDA-Funded Industrial Parks— 1968-74.* Washington, D.C., 1974.

Environmental Protection Agency, Unpublished working documents on the status of projects funded but uncompleted. Washington, D.C., June 11, 1980.

Executive Office of the President, "Small Community and Rural Development Policy," Washington, D.C., December 20, 1979.

Executive Office of the President, Office of Management and Budget, *Managing Federal Assistance in the 1980s,* Washington, D.C., March, 1980.

Executive Office of the President, Office of Management and Budget, *Public Works as Countercyclical Assistance.* Washington, D.C., November, 1979.

Executive Office of the President, Office of Management and Budget. *Reorganization Study of Local Development Assistance Programs,* Washington, D.C., December, 1978.

Executive Office of the President, Office of Management and Budget, *Special Analyses. Budget of the United States Government—Fiscal Year 1980.* Washington, D.C., 1980.

The Federal City Council, *Local Public Infrastructure in the District of Columbia.* Washington, D.C., August, 1980.

Getzels, Judith and Thurow, Charles. *Local Capital Improvements and Development Management: Analyses and Case Studies.* American Planning Association, Chicago, Illinois. June, 1980.

Grossman, David A., *The Future of New York City's Capital Plan,* The Urban Institute, Washington, D.C., 1979.

Grossman, David A., *Water Resources Priorities for the Northeast,* The consortium of Northeast Organizations, Washington, D.C., September, 1979.

Hatry, Harry, P., *Local Government Capital Infrastructure Planning: Current State-of-the-Art and "State-of-the-Practice."* The Urban Institute, Washington, D.C., 1980.

Hoyle, Robert S. "Capital Budgeting Models and Planning: An Evolutionary Process," Managerial Planning, November/December, 1978.

Hubbel, Kenneth L., editor, *Fiscal Crisis in American Cities: The Federal Response.* Ballinger Publishing Company, Cambridge, Massachusetts, 1979.

93

Humphrey, Nancy; Peterson, George E.; and Wilson, Peter. *The Future of Cincinnati's Capital Plant.* The Urban Institute, Washington, D.C., 1979.

Humphrey, Nancy; Peterson, George E.; and Wilson, Peter. *The Future of Cleveland's Capital Plant.* The Urban Institute, Washington, D.C., 1979.

Industrial Research and Extension Center, *Effects of Environmental Protection Regulation on Regional Economic Development,* University of Arkansas, Little Rock, Arkansas, September, 1977.

Joint Economic Committee of the Congress of the United States, 96th Congress, 2nd Session. *Public Works as a Countercyclical Tool,* 1980.

Kaynor, Edward R. "Uncertainty in Water Resources Planning in the Connecticut River Basin." American Water Resources Association, December, 1978.

Lapping, Mark B., "The State of Water Resources Planning and Management in New England: An Overview of Institutional Frameworks and Issues." The New England Federal Regional Council, Boston, Massachusetts, October, 1980.

Malone, Larry. *Coordinating State Functional Planning Programs: Strategies for Balancing Conflicting Objectives.* U.S. Department of Housing and Urban Development, Washington, D.C., 1977.

Milkman, Raymond H. and Toborg, Mary A., *Evaluating Economic Development Programs.* The Lazar Institute, Washington, D.C., 1978.

Morrison, Peter A., "Overview of Demographic Trends Shaping the Nation's Future." The Rand Paper Series, The Rand Corporation, Santa Monica, California, May, 1978.

National Conference of State Legislatures and the National Governor's Association, "Statement on Federalism Reform." November 25, 1980.

National Governors' Association, *Federal Roadblocks to Efficient State Government,* 1977.

National Governors' Association Center for Policy Research, *Bypassing the States: Wrong Turn on Urban Aid.* Washington, D.C., November, 1979.

Newman, William H. and Logan, James P., *Strategy, Policy and Central Management.* Southwestern Publishing Company, Dallas, Texas, 1976.

Oklahoma Water Resources Board, Oklahoma Comprehensive Water Plan, Oklahoma City, Oklahoma, April, 1980.

Pagano, Michael and Moore, Richard J. "Emerging Issues in Financing Basic Infra-structure," unpublished paper, September, 1980.

Pritchard, Allen, E., "Private Delivery of Public Services," The Academy for Contemporary Problems, Columbus, Ohio, 1976.

Reuss, Henry, S. *To Save Our Cities,* Public Affairs Press, Washington, D.C., Washington, D.C., 1977.

Salamon, Lester M., "In Pursuit of Reorganization: The Question of Goals," paper given at the Administrative Conference of the United States, Washington, D.C., 1980.

Schramm, Gunter, *The Value of Time in Environmental Decision Processes.* The University of Michigan, Ann Arbor, Michigan. November, 1979.

Schwartz, Gail Garfield and Choate, Pat. *Being Number One: Rebuilding the U.S. Economy.* Lexington Books, Lexington, Massachusetts, 1980.

Schwertz, Eddie L. Jr., *The Local Growth Management Guidebook.* The Southern Growth Policies Board, Washington, D.C., 1979.

Snelling, Governor Richard A., *Policy Statement on Capital Debt,* State of Vermont, February, 1979.

Stamm, Charles F. and Howell, James M. *Urban Fiscal Stress: A Comparative Analysis of 66 U.S. Cities.* Touche Ross and Company and The First National Bank of Boston, Boston, Massachusetts, 1979.

State of Colorado, *Private Choices, Public Strategies,* Denver, Colorado, February, 1980.

Steiner, George A., *Top Management Planning.* The MacMillian Company, New York City, 1969.

Subcommittee on Economic Development of the Committee on Public Works and Transportation of the House of Representatives, Ninety-Fourth Congress, 1st Session. *Public Works Project and Program Acceleration.* Washington, D.C., March 12, 1975.

Subcommittee on Economic Growth and Stabilization of the Joint Economic Committee of the Congress of the United States, 96th Congress, 1st Session, *Deteriorating Infrastructure in Urban and Rural Areas,* Washington, D.C., 1979.

Subcommittee on the City of the Committee on Banking, Finance and Urban Affairs, House of Representatives, 95th Congress, 2nd Session. *Small Cities: How Can the Federal and State Governments Response to Their Diverse Needs?* Washington, D.C., May, 1978.

The Urban Consortium, "Urban Infrastructure: Assessing Its Condition and Developing Policies and Methods for the Future." Washington, D.C., July, 1980.

U.S. Bureau of the Census, *Statistical Abstract of the United States: 1979.* (100 edition.) Washington, D.C., 1979.

U.S. Department of Agriculture, Rural Development Progress, January 1977-June 1979. Washington, D.C., 1979.

U.S. Department of Agriculture, *Social and Economic Trends in Rural America,* Washington, D.C., October, 1979.

U.S. Department of Commerce, "Establishment of a National Development Bank" National Public Advisory Committee on Regional Economic Development. Washington, D.C., 1976.

U.S. Department of Commerce, *Industrial Location Determinants,* Washington, D.C., 1973.

U.S. Department of Commerce, Industry and Trade Administration, *1980, U.S. Industrial Outlook,* Washington, D.C., 1980.

U.S. Department of Housing and Urban Development, *Advance Project Planning for Public Works: A Systematic Approach.* Washington, D.C., 1979.

U.S. Department of Housing and Urban Development. "Causes and Consequences of Delay in Implementing the Community Development Block Grant Program," Washington, D.C., June, 1980.

U.S. Department of Housing and Urban Development, "Streamlining Land Use Regulation: What Local Public Officials Should Know." Washington, D.C., 1980.

U.S. Department of Housing and Urban Development, *The President's National Urban Policy Report.* Washington, D.C., 1980.

U.S. Department of Transportation, *Draft Transportation Agenda for the 1980s: The Issues,* Washington, D.C., March, 1980.

U.S. Department of Transportation, Federal Highway Administration, *1981 Federal Highway Legislation:* Program and Revenue Options, Washington, D.C., June, 1980.

U.S. Environmental Protection Agency, *Clean Water: Fact Sheet,* Washington, D.C., April, 1980.

U.S. Environmental Protection Agency, *The Cost of Clean Air and Water: A Report to the Congress.* Washington, D.C., August, 1979.

U.S. General Accounting Office, *Federal Capital Budgeting: A Collection of Haphazard Practices.* Washington, D.C., February, 1981.

U.S. General Accounting Office, *Federally Assisted Areawide Planning Need to Simplify Policies and Practices,* Washington, D.C., March, 1977.

U.S. General Accounting Office, *Foresighted Planning and Budgeting Needed for Public Buildings Program.* Washington, D.C., September 9, 1980.

U.S. General Accounting Office, *Long-Range Analysis Activities in Seven Federal Agencies.* Washington, D.C., December, 1976.

U.S. General Accounting Office, *More Can Be Done to Insure that Industrial Parks Create New Jobs,* Washington, D.C., December 2, 1980.

U.S. General Accounting Office, *Perspectives on Intergovernmental Policy and Fiscal Relations.* Washington, D.C., June 28, 1979.

U.S. Senate, 96th Congress, 2nd Session S. 2080 (a draft bill), Washington, D.C., June 12, 1980.

U.S. Senate, 96th Congress, 2nd Session, *Standing Rules of the Senate,* Washington, D.C., March 25, 1980.

Vaughan, Roger J., "Countercyclical Public Works: A Rational Alternative." Testimony given before the Joint Economic Committee of the United States Congress, June 17, 1980. Washington, D.C.

Vaughan, Roger J., *Public Works as a Countercyclical Device: A Review of the Issues.* The Rand Corporation, Santa Monica, California, July, 1976.

Vernez, Georges and Vaughan Roger, J., *Assessment of Countercyclical Public Works and Public Service Employment Programs,* The Rand Corporation, Santa Monica, California, 1978.

Vernez, Georges; Vaughan, Roger, J.; and Yin, Robert K., *Federal Activities in Urban Economic Development.* The Rand Corporation, April, 1979.

Vernez, Georges; Vaughan, Roger, J.; Burright, Burke; and Coleman, Sinclair. *Regional Cycles and Employment Effects of Public Works Investments.* The Rand Corporation, Santa Monica, California, 1977.

Wallace, Holly, "Infrastructured: Maintain It Now or Pay the Price Tomorrow" *City Economic Development,* The National League of Cities, May 12, 1980.

White House Conference on Balanced National Growth, *Proceedings,* Washington, D.C., 1978.

Wildavsky, Aaron, Budgeting: *A Comparative Theory of Budgetary Processes,* Little, Brown and Company. Boston, Massachusetts, 1975.

Wilson, Peter. *The Future of Dallas's Capital Plant,* The Urban Institute, Washington, D.C., 1980.

INDEX

Productivity decline, 11
Property tax, 85
Public infrastructure, deteriorating condition of, 1-9. *See also* Public works; Public works investments
Public utility carry-overs, 42
Public works: administrative waste and, 59, 61–66; allocating responsibility for, 63–65, 78–81, 82–85; assessing the condition of, 4, 7; backlog of, 27–28, 33, 42, 47, 50–51, 73, 87; state-local budgets and, 26; construction industry and, 12, 15; construction versus maintenance of, 33–34, 62, 70, 71–72, 83–84; coordination of, 63–66; as counter-cyclical device, 24–28, 69, 73; "crisis" management of, 25–26; data on, 59, 73; demographics and, 73; employment and, 11, 12, 15, 17, 24, 26–28; evaluation of, 74; financing of, 33–38, 71, 73, 74; fraud and, 56–59; influence of, on private firms, 17; inventory of, 1–4; national importance of, 9, 11; new technology and, 73; operation and maintenance expenditures of, 70–71; places and, 15, 17, 32–33; regional needs and, 26, 28, 84; setting priorities among, 33, 34; as supply side investments, 11. *See also* Public infrastructure; Public works investments
Public Works Impact Program (PWIP), 24, 26–27
Public works investments, 1–9, 30–31, 33; choosing goals and objectives for, 72–73; as economic tool, 17, 24–28; mandated, 82–83; personnel policies of, 74; pro-cyclical pattern of, 17, 24, 25; research and analysis of, 73–74; targeting of, 27–28. *See also* Public infrastructure; Public works

Railroads, deterioration of, 2
Recession, and public works investments, 17, 24, 26, 27
Reconstruction Finance Corporation, 34–35

Regional variations, and public works programs, 26, 28, 84
Regulation of state and local actions, 80
Revenue sharing, 25, 80–81, 83
Rural areas, public works in, 3, 33
Rural Facilities Simplification Process, 64

Saint Louis, 4, 7
San Bernardino, delays in public works construction, 47
Seattle, dispute mediation in, 53–54
Smithsonian Air and Space Museum, 40
Special Analysis, to accompany annual budget, 87
Special interest groups, 81
State capital planning, 85
Steel industry, 17
Strategic management techniques, 74
Streets, deterioration of, 7
Study of Public Works Investment in the United States, 69

Tennessee, 56–57
Tennessee Valley Authority (TVA), 40, 47
Texas panhandle, 3
Time management, 51–55
Triggering devices data, 88
Two-step funding, 53

Unemployment rate, 17
U.S. capital budget, 68–73, 74–76, 87–88
User charges, to finance public works, 34, 35–36

Waco, capital construction policy in, 70–71
Washington, D.C., water program in, 35
Water pollution control standards, 2
Water resource development, 3
Water supply facilities, 2, 3, 7; funding for, 83; and user charges, 35–36
Water treatment plants, 15

Zero-Based Budgeting (ZBB), 74–75

Pat Choate is a Senior Policy Analyst for Economics at TRW Inc. Prior to joining TRW he was a Visiting Federal Fellow at the Academy for Contemporary Problems. Dr. Choate has worked in a wide array of policy and management positions in the Federal and State Governments. He has held positions in the United States Department of Commerce's Economic Development Administration as Director of the Office of Economic Research and as Regional Director for the Appalachian and Southern Regional Offices. Previously, he worked as Commissioner of Economic and Community Development for the State of Tennessee and as Director of State Planning for the State of Oklahoma.

Dr. Choate is the author of many papers and reports on development, economic policy, and public administration. Most recently he co-authored *Being Number One: Rebuilding the U.S. Economy* (Lexington Books), and he is the author of *As Time Goes By: The Costs and Consequences of Delay* (The Academy for Contemporary Problems).

Dr. Choate holds a Ph.D. in economics from the University of Oklahoma.

Susan Walter is Manager for State Government Issues at the General Electric Company. Prior to joining General Electric, Ms. Walter was the Associate Director for Executive Management of The Council of State Planning Agencies, an affiliate organization of The National Governors' Association.

Ms. Walter has had diverse experience in the analysis and management of public policy issues for both the legislative and executive branches of government and for this publication has concentrated on applying strategic planning and management to public sector management problems. As part of this project she was the primary staff person for the White House Conference on Strategic Planning and edited its *Proceedings*. The project also included the publication of a series of books on state management issues and technical assistance to state Governors' offices and agencies.

Before her association with The Council of State Planning Agencies, Ms. Walter was a Special Assistant to Governor Reubin Askew and the Executive Director of the Florida Advisory Council on Intergovernmental Relations. In addition, she has held senior staff positions for both the Florida House of Representatives and Senate in human services and appropriations.

Ms. Walter received her masters degree from the Maxwell School of Syracuse University.